MICHAEL MENSING – RAILWAY PHOTOGRAPHER

VOLUME 2

THE WEST MIDLANDS 1959

RCTS PUBLICATIONS

rcts.org.uk

ISBN 978-1-7391324-4-6

Published by The Railway Correspondence and Travel Society,
16 Welby Close, Maidenhead SL6 3PY, United Kingdom.

Printed by Ackent Media, UK

Typesetting and page layout by RCTS Members

INTRODUCTION

This book is the second in the series that the Railway Correspondence & Travel Society is producing showcasing the work of renowned photographer Michael Mensing (1933-2014). This follows on from Volume 1 published in 2021 which introduced Michael to the public by way of a sample of his colour photography covering the whole of the UK.

Michael was raised in Solihull and worked for the Midland Bank in Birmingham before transferring in 1979 to a branch at Fareham in Hampshire. Michael was a lover of rural locations and incorporated scenery into his pictures. Unlike many of his contemporaries, he did not visit engine sheds to take static locomotive portraits and he took only a few pictures at large stations. Although he took standard three-quarter views of trains, many of his pictures used other viewpoints such as 'going-away' and 'panned' shots and they often included local points of interest both within and outside the railway boundary. Michael took his first few tentative steps with colour photography in 1956 and increasingly used the format during 1957 and 1958, but it was not until 1959 that he started to use colour more regularly.

This second volume covers his native West Midlands during 1959 when dieselisation was under way, but at that date almost entirely on suburban services. However, in contrast to most other photographers of that era, Michael diligently recorded the new diesel multiple units as well as the steam scene.

This picture was a self-portrait that Michael took when testing his first camera purchased with 21st birthday money in 1954. This fact was recorded in his notebook for that period as well as the later results from other similar tests. Once satisfied with the outcome he then would start using that camera. It is clear from his notebooks that he habitually went out with both black & white and colour film loaded in his various cameras.

With his home in Solihull, it was almost inevitable that he took more photographs on the Western Region lines than on those of the London Midland Region; most were in the greater Birmingham area with a relatively small number around Wolverhampton. Many pictures were taken after he arrived back from the city in the early evening although he did take a few in the morning rush hour before he went to work. The glamour was provided by Collett's Kings which were undergoing a renaissance after they had been fitted with double blastpipes and chimneys, and they were ably supported by his Castle Class. The ubiquitous mixed traffic Halls appeared on freight, parcels and passenger trains, and the GWR 2-6-2Ts and 43xx Class 2-6-0s were clinging on to some of the suburban trains into Birmingham; Michael's portfolio also covered the through and local trip freights.

In 1959 there was still the opportunity for him to photograph the procession of summer Saturday holiday specials between the Midlands and the south and south west seaside towns. Michael also recorded the everyday weekday scene with its mix of freights, expresses and local trains on the London Midland Region as well as the Western. After BR encouraged its Regions to take on more of their own identities in 1956, the Western's Works at Swindon began painting almost any engine which might conceivably work a passenger train in green, while 'chocolate and cream' livery was reintroduced on the named expresses, and the use of colour film allowed this to be captured.

This book is arranged with the pictures in date order to produce a photographic journey of Michael's regular visits to his favourite West Midlands locations during 1959.

The DMUs are described with their builders' details since they were built in the late 1950s long before the TOPS classifications were introduced but, to help the readers more familiar with the latter, these have been included in the first captions for each type.

The RCTS Publications team which produced the book took advantage of the largest national railway enthusiast society by tapping into the depth of local knowledge in the West Midlands to provide much interesting detail on the locations and train workings.

John Jennison, Editor

ACKNOWLEDGEMENTS

Grateful thanks go to caption contributors Steve Burdett, Bob Dalton, Robert Darlaston, Nick Daunt and Peter Fortune, and to Steve Batty and Patrick Bennett who prepared the images ready for publication.

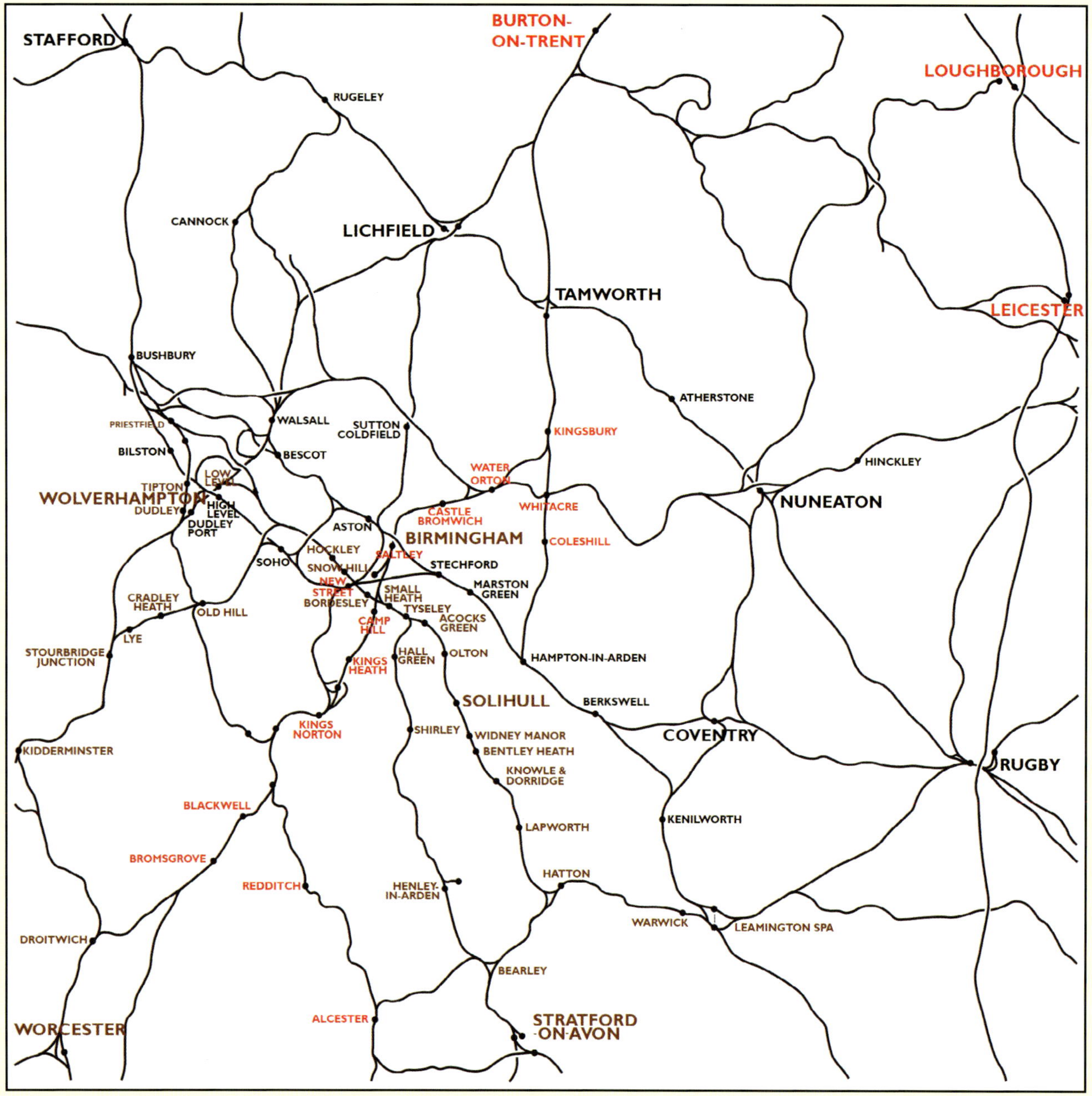

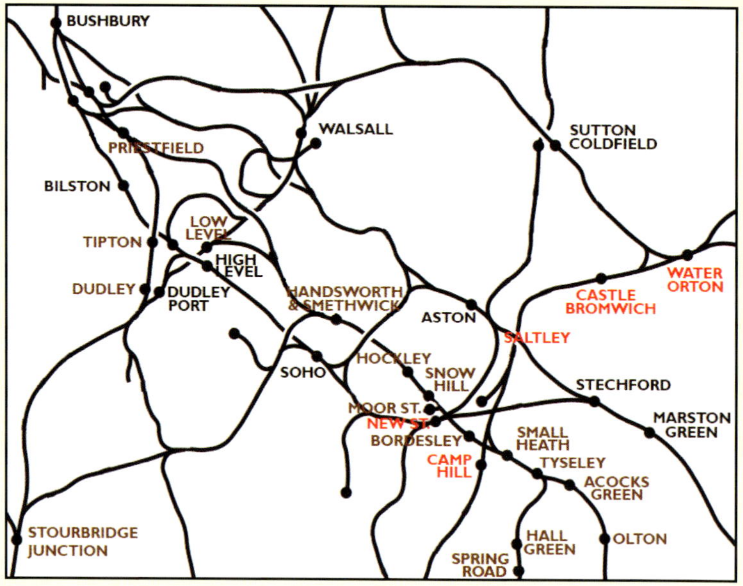

These simplified maps show the lines and locations where Michael took the photographs used in this book. The stations are coloured to show the original pre-1923 company: black for the LNWR, red for the Midland Railway and brown for the Great Western.

The lines in the north of the area around Birmingham and Wolverhampton are complex and therefore these are shown in more detail on the larger scale insert above.

The red glass in the lamp affixed to the buffer-beam of Collett 61xx 2-6-2T 6116 indicates that it was propelling its short train, an Up ballast or similar working, at Widney Manor on the relief lines towards Knowle & Dorridge on Sunday 26th April 1959. Apparently, there was engineering work at or near Knowle & Dorridge on that day. To minimise disruption of traffic, this sort of work was normally carried out on a Sunday. 6116 would usually have been employed on Birmingham commuter trains, but on Sundays the reduced service required fewer engines. The 61xx class had been synonymous with Paddington suburban services since the early 1930s, but 6116 was one of six transferred from various Thames Valley depots to Tyseley in October 1953. They were replacements for newly-built BR Standard Class 3 2-6-2Ts which had been found unsatisfactory for the demanding Birmingham suburban trains and were moved to South Wales. 6116 stayed at Tyseley until July 1962 when it was transferred to Fishguard.

Stechford is the second intermediate station out of Birmingham New Street on the London Midland Region line to Euston. It had a junction which connected it with Aston on the old Grand Junction route that was used by many freight trains and was a vital diversionary route for passenger trains from the West Coast Main Line when there was engineering work between Rugby and Stafford. Stechford also had a large goods yard which handled a considerable amount of domestic coal traffic, as shown by the line of 16T mineral wagons in the background. A three-car Birmingham Railway Carriage & Wagon Co. DMU (later Class 104), with Driving Motor Composite M50504 leading and an extra trailer coach in the consist, arrives at Stechford on Tuesday 28th April 1959 with the 1.40pm Birmingham New Street-Rugby service. These were one of the most numerous of the first generation DMU classes with over 300 vehicles built by BRC&W at its Smethwick factory.

The trees are in full blossom in this lovely spring scene as BR Standard Class 4 4-6-0 75026 and King 4-6-0 6020 *King Henry IV* double-head the 5.10pm Paddington-Wolverhampton near Widney Manor on Tuesday 28th April 1959. The picture was taken near the Hillfield Road underbridge just to the north of the station. The King, which had been at Stafford Road since January 1949, was quite capable of working this heavy train unaided and 75026 may have been attached to the train, perhaps at Leamington (the train's only intermediate stop), to save a light engine movement. 75026 was allocated to Tyseley, having arrived from Chester shed on 11th April, but moved away to Machynlleth on 11th May 1959.

Michael took many pictures on the Western Region around Acocks Green and South Yardley. One of his favourite vantage points was the Woodcock Lane overbridge just beyond the London end of the station. This is a typical steam-hauled suburban service, the 5.38pm Birmingham Snow Hill-Knowle & Dorridge, leaving there with Class 61xx 2-6-2T 6139, on Thursday 30th April 1959. By this date, most of the local commuter services were worked by DMUs, but steam could still be seen during the morning and evening peak periods. The train is on the Up relief line, just south of Acocks Green & South Yardley station. The splitting signal controls entrance to the Down goods loop, which began just behind the camera. 6139 was another of the half-dozen of the class transferred to Tyseley in 1953 to replace the BR Standard Class 3 tanks. Note the First Class compartments in the front coach.

Twenty or so minutes later that same day we see another steam-hauled local from the Woodcock Lane vantage point, the 6.5pm Birmingham Snow Hill-Leamington Spa, hauled by Churchward 43xx 2-6-0 6332. This train was known as 'the Six-Five Special' after a television programme of that name, devoted to popular music, which was broadcast at that time on Saturdays between February 1957 and December 1958. The train, which had acquired something of a cult status among enthusiasts, was one of several steam-hauled evening Up commuter services from Snow Hill. It ran fast to Tyseley, arriving at 6.12pm and was due at Acocks Green at 6.15pm and Leamington Spa at 6.55pm. It was almost always hauled by a Mogul, usually from Stourbridge Junction shed like 6332, which was there from April 1952 until withdrawal in September 1960. Numbers 6332 and 6349 were the engines of choice since it was said they were the only ones which could keep time.

A third picture taken from the Woodcock Lane overbridge near Acocks Green as the evening shadows lengthen on Thursday 30th April 1959, a freight on the Up Main line headed by Large Prairie 4171. This engine was one of the final batch of the 5101 Class 2-6-2Ts, numbers 4160-79 built by British Railways in 1948-49. They were equally at home working freight as well as passenger trains and six of the twenty were allocated to the West Midland sheds at Leamington, Tyseley and Stourbridge. 4171 was built in 1949 and spent almost all its life allocated to Leamington, from where it was withdrawn in October 1964.

Michael lived in Solihull, so it is not surprising that many of his photographs were taken either at Solihull station itself or at various locations in the vicinity. With the houses in Dorchester Road in the background, 4974 *Talgarth Hall* approaches the station with an Up Class K freight on Thursday 30th April 1959. It is in lined green livery with the final BR crest. A Tyseley engine between November 1958 and April 1960, 4974 was withdrawn from Gloucester Horton Road in April 1962.

43xx 2-6-0 6349 starts the 'Six-Five Special', the 6.5pm Birmingham Snow Hill-Leamington Spa, away from Widney Manor station on Saturday 2nd May 1959. 6349 was built in May 1923 and was transferred to Stourbridge Junction from Gloucester Horton Road in November 1957, remaining there until the end of 1960. This picture gives a good general impression of Widney Manor station as well as showing the housing estates that had been built nearby.

Michael regularly visited Stechford around lunch time, including this one taken from the Station Road overbridge looking east towards Coventry. LMS Stanier 8F 2-8-0 48681 was shunting freight onto the Up Slow line on Monday 4th May 1959. The engine, which was allocated to Toton shed near Nottingham from new until August 1965, was one of the 8Fs built during the Second World War by the Southern Railway, at Brighton in January 1944. Appropriately, the brake van leading is of Southern Railway origin. The empty 16T steel mineral wagon next to it may well have deposited its load of domestic coal at Stechford. The standard ex-LNWR signal box visible in the background is Stechford No.1, which controlled movements at the east end of the station; the main Birmingham New Street-Coventry line is on the right of the picture. On the left is the Parkinson Cowan factory which made gas cookers on this site until 1995.

43xx Class 2-6-0 7317 heads an Up Class K freight towards Solihull station on Monday 4th May 1959. This may well be the same working as that seen in the previous week (on page 7) and the location is almost identical. 7317 had recently been transferred from Tyseley to Stourbridge shed. Solihull's large goods shed is on the extreme right.

A change of viewpoint at Acocks Green and South Yardley: Michael had taken up a position on the Sherbourne Road overbridge which was part of the Birmingham Outer Circle Ring Road, looking in the Down direction towards Tyseley. The station entrance building is sited on this bridge, behind the photographer. The train on Thursday 7th May 1959 was a well-filled morning commuter service, the 8.37am ex-Solihull, the 8.23 Lapworth to Handsworth & Smethwick, headed by Tyseley's 5101 Class 2-6-2T 4170, another of the BR-built engines. The train is on the Down Main line, and the four tracks were, from left to right, Down Relief, Up Relief, Down Main, Up Main. The two Main lines diverged to accommodate one of the station's two island platforms. The bridge in the distance, carrying Rookwood Road, was another of Michael's regular vantage points (see pages 23 and 24). Except for two years at Leamington Spa in 1955-56, 4170 was a Tyseley engine from new in October 1949 until withdrawal in August 1961.

Wolverhampton Stafford Road's Castle Class 4-6-0 5070 *Sir Daniel Gooch* departs from Stratford-on-Avon with the northbound "Cornishman" to Wolverhampton Low Level on Saturday 23rd May 1959. Originally intended to carry the name *Bridgwater Castle* which had been on Castle 5045 until September 1937, instead it became *Sir Daniel Gooch*; 5070 had been at Stafford Road since 1940. The fact that Michael described this as 'the main part' of the train suggests that the Kingswear portion, which was normally combined with the Penzance portion at Exeter St. David's, was working as a separate train on that day. Stratford is no longer a through station, services from Birmingham terminating there. The important cross-country route to Cheltenham via Honeybourne was severed in 1976, although part of it is now operated as a heritage line by the Gloucestershire Warwickshire Steam Railway. The building towering over the tender in the background is that of Flowers brewery and the chimney is part of the gasworks complex. The gasworks sidings were notable for the stabling of the Royal Train during visits to the town.

The 12.42pm Coventry-Birmingham New Street at Stechford station on Tuesday 16th June 1959, hauled by BR Standard Class 4 2-6-4T 80084 from Bletchley shed. At this period, this seems to have been a regular turn for a Bletchley Standard tank. Presumably, the engine had worked to Rugby or Coventry on another train and then been 'borrowed' for a trip to New Street and back, before returning to its home shed. Bletchley had eight of these engines on its books, but there were none at any of the London Midland Region sheds in the Birmingham area. Those locals which were still steam-hauled were usually worked by ex-LMS 2-6-4 tanks of Stanier or Fairburn design, Ivatt 2-6-2 tanks or Ivatt Class 2 2-6-0s. 80084 was allocated to Bletchley from new in May 1954, but by the end of 1959 it had been transferred to Bricklayers Arms on the Southern Region where it survived until 1965. The timber station building in the background was, like that at Acocks Green & South Yardley, situated on the Birmingham Outer Circle Ring Road. Note the wooden-bodied open wagons in the goods yard on the left, with the Parkinson Cowan factory beyond.

The Down platform at Stechford had a water crane at the Birmingham end and the No.2 signal box was separated from the platform by the exit road from the Down loop. The junction with the Aston line which curved away to the right was around 150 yards beyond the signal box; the line to New Street is on the left. The Up platform gave a good view of the Up goods yard which differed from the Down yard in that little shunting was done there, except that needed to serve Cartwright & Co (Timber Merchants and Importers), the coal yard and the common user dock. The yard was also used to drop-off single or small rakes of pre-sorted wagons to be picked up by other trains, and it was common to have rakes of engineers' wagons in the yard for lengthy periods of time.

LMS Hughes-Fowler 5MT 2-6-0 42923 was taking water standing at the west end of platform 2 on 16th June 1959. These engines were known as 'Crabs' because it was thought that their noticeably inclined cylinders, with the running plate raised over them, gave them an ungainly appearance not helped by their LMS 'Old Standard' 3,500 gallon tenders, which were narrower than the engines. 42923 was built at Crewe in November 1930 as LMS 13223 and withdrawn in January 1964 after 33 years in service.

42923 was allocated to Longsight, Manchester, between July 1941 and November 1960 and was probably heading for home, since it is signalled to take the Aston route. It is surprising that the road has already been set, meaning that no trains from the New Street direction could run east across the junction while the engine was still taking water. This was, after all, a busy route.

The 1.40pm Birmingham New Street-Rugby arrives at Stechford station on Tuesday 16th June 1959. The train consists of two two-car Birmingham Railway Carriage & Wagon Co. DMUs with Driving Motor Brake Second M50533 leading. The platform buildings, which are in deep shadow, are of typical LNWR design timber construction. The two island platforms were accessed from the road by stairs. In the distance is Stechford Junction with its array of signals, which was the scene of a severe accident in February 1967 when the 13.15 Manchester Piccadilly-Coventry service with an AM4 EMU, 026, hit BR Sulzer Type 2 D5002 which had been allowed onto the main line whilst running round a ballast train resulting in the deaths of nine passengers and injuries to 16 others.

Another picture of the 'Six Five Special' (the 6.5pm Birmingham Snow Hill-Leamington Spa) leaving Acocks Green and South Yardley station hauled by Stourbridge Junction's 43xx 2-6-0 6349, this time on Tuesday 16th June 1959. From here the train called at all stations, but it still reached Leamington in a creditable 50 minutes. In this 'going-away shot' we can appreciate how little protection from the elements the Churchward cab gave the footplate crew. The first coach is a 1st/2nd Composite and like all the suburban trains on this route since the early 1930s, the train consisted entirely of GWR design 60ft. length non-corridor coaches. 6349 is standing by platform 1 which was normally used by express services but because of the heavy commuter traffic out of Birmingham this local had to use the Up Main. Less than ten minutes earlier the 5.52pm from Snow Hill would have stopped at platform 3 on the Up Relief line, while the 6.0pm departure, the 2.25pm express from Birkenhead to Paddington, raced through on the Up Main. Hard on the heels of the 6.5pm would be the 6.25pm stopping service from Moor Street.

We return to the Woodcock Lane overbridge near Acocks Green and South Yardley station, but this time we are looking in the Down direction, towards the station and its signal box. About to be overtaken by a DMU on the Up Main, a heavy Class K freight was approaching on the Up Relief headed by Churchward Class 28xx 2-8-0 2816 from Banbury shed on Tuesday 16th June 1959. Much, probably all, of the train consists of loaded coal wagons. 2816 had been built at Swindon in December 1905 but was destined only to survive another four months after this picture was taken and was withdrawn in October 1959. The track on the extreme left is the Down goods loop where freight trains were held to allow passenger trains to pass. The area is more heavily built up nowadays and only two tracks remain.

Another picture taken from the Woodcock Lane overbridge on Tuesday 16th June 1959. 4175, one of the BR-built 5101 Class 2-6-2Ts, is approaching Acocks Green station with the 8.28am Solihull-Birmingham Snow Hill. This final batch of Large Prairies were originally painted unlined black as pictured, but some of them later acquired lined green livery. The Down goods loop can clearly be seen. At this time in the morning the sun was right for taking pictures in this direction. 4175 was allocated to Kidderminster shed until September 1964 when it was transferred to Stourbridge Junction from where it was withdrawn in October 1965, one of the last GWR design Prairie tanks in service.

Michael was standing on the Up Relief platform at Acocks Green and South Yardley to take this picture of BR Class 9F 2-10-0 92139 passing with a Down Class D part-fitted freight on Wednesday 17th June 1959. It was allocated to Saltley, the principal ex-Midland Railway shed in Birmingham and was one of nineteen 9Fs there at this time. It is likely that this was an inter-regional working, probably to Washwood Heath yard which would gain access to the ex-Midland Camp Hill line at Bordesley Junction, where it crossed the GWR route by means of an overbridge. The soot deposit on the side of the overbridge is from engines of stopping trains where they came to a stand on the Up Relief.

Hatton is on the Birmingham Snow Hill-Paddington line, situated near the summit of an incline by which Down trains climb out of the Avon valley onto the West Midland plateau. Just to the north of the station is a triangular junction, hidden by the train in this picture, where the original line to Stratford-on-Avon diverges from the London route. Stafford Road's 6017 *King Edward IV* was nearing the top of the bank with the 5.10pm Paddington-Wolverhampton Low Level on Thursday 18th June 1959. 6017 arrived at Wolverhampton Stafford Road from Laira in February 1959 ousted by the arrival of the Warship diesel-hydraulics, remaining there until withdrawal in July 1962 when Western class diesels were being introduced on the Birmingham line expresses. In the foreground is Milepost 112¾, mileage on this route was still measured according to the original 'Great Way Round' via Reading, Didcot and Oxford. This train would have used the cut-off via High Wycombe and Bicester, by which this point would be about 94 miles from Paddington. In the distance it is possible to make out Hatton station itself, and haymaking was in progress in the field to the left.

At the same location near Hatton a few minutes later, Hall Class 4-6-0 5963 *Wimpole Hall* passes with the 3.18pm Paddington-Wolverhampton Low Level. This was a curious train, routed via Oxford, and after calling at several stations between Paddington and Didcot, it was all stations to Oxford, then Heyford, Banbury, Leamington Spa, Birmingham Snow Hill before it finally reached Wolverhampton at 8.25pm. 5963 was allocated to Westbury shed and had probably been borrowed by Old Oak Common to work to Wolverhampton and back before returning to the West Country. The second vehicle of the train is a green-liveried Southern Railway Utility van and ahead of it is a horsebox. On the adjacent track is a train of vans, one of which carries a Blue Circle Cement label. The underbridge in the foreground appears to have undergone some recent strengthening.

Michael's third picture in the evening of Thursday 18th June 1959 near Milepost 112¾ north of Hatton, is of Old Oak Common's Hall Class 4-6-0 6942 *Eshton Hall* on a parcels train, the 12.55pm from West London to Shrewsbury. Behind, is a train of iron ore hoppers. This route carried a considerable amount of iron ore traffic, originating from the quarries in Oxfordshire and Northamptonshire, and bound for the furnaces of the Black Country or, continuing via Stourbridge Junction, Worcester, Hereford and Newport, for South Wales.

Viewed from Rookwood Road bridge, Acocks Green with the houses of Alexander Road bordering, WD Austerity 2-8-0 90268 was running under clear signals on the Up Main with a lengthy Class H coal train on Friday 19th June 1959. These engines were designed by Robin Riddles for the Ministry of Supply and after the war, British Railways acquired 733 of them. A Southall engine since March 1951, 90268 was transferred to Banbury in July 1959. The train has no fewer than three brake vans and also includes a solitary Conflat wagon with a container. The overbridge in the distance is that carrying Stockfield Road and beyond it is the junction with the North Warwickshire line and Tyseley station. The GWR wooden signal posts hold the Tyseley Intermediate Home and Acocks Green Distant signals. The slopes of the cutting show evidence of recent fires.

We are now looking in the opposite direction from the Rookwood Road overbridge. The Sherbourne Road overbridge is in the distance, with the end of the Acocks Green & South Yardley station entrance building just visible on the extreme right. A three-car Derby-built suburban DMU (Class 116 under TOPS) was passing on the Down Main, forming the 12.57pm Stratford-Birmingham Snow Hill, on Friday 19th June 1959. 29 units of this type were delivered to Tyseley in 1957 for the suburban services from Snow Hill and Moor Street and were introduced to the public with an extensive publicity campaign. These high-density, non-gangwayed units were painted in unlined dark green relieved only by the 'speed whiskers' on the cab front and the white dome on the roof. The 12.57pm was one of a handful of workings to travel from Stratford-upon-Avon to Birmingham via Claverdon, rather than the more usual North Warwickshire line.

Marston Green on the line to Coventry, Rugby and Euston is approximately 6¼ miles from Birmingham New Street. Before the station was remodelled during the 1960s in connection with electrification, there was a level crossing worked from the station's signal box. The station itself was a standard ex-LNWR wooden structure. Michael had chosen a spot, much loved by the spotters of the day, alongside the level crossing gates, to take this picture of a two-car Metro-Cammell DMU arriving as the 5.39pm Rugby Midland-Birmingham New Street on Friday 19th June 1959. Fifteen of these units were delivered to the LMR from the factory at Washwood Heath, Birmingham between October 1958 and January 1959. They were based at Monument Lane depot and used on local services between New Street, Coventry, Rugby and Leamington. Classed as 101 under TOPS, the Metro-Cammell units were probably the best and amongst the longest-lived of the first generation DMUs and the last one was not withdrawn until 2003. Alongside the Home signal, which is 'off' for the DMU, is the Down goods loop, together with the crossover giving access to a coal yard where a 16-ton steel-bodied mineral wagon is just visible. In the distance, looking towards Hampton-in-Arden, are two overbridges, known locally as First Bridge and Second Bridge.

This picture was taken from the fourth overbridge east of Marston Green on Friday 19th June 1959. Today, that bridge is at the west end of Birmingham International station (opened in 1976), and the surrounding area is completely built-up, with Birmingham Airport and the National Exhibition Centre close by. The train is the Down "Midlander", the 5.40pm from Euston to Wolverhampton High Level, usually a Jubilee turn, but on this occasion was hauled by two Stanier Class 5 4-6-0s, 44807 piloting 45405. The former was allocated to Monument Lane shed at Birmingham between September 1958 and June 1960, and the latter was at Bushbury, the LMR shed at Wolverhampton, from October 1943 until April 1965.

Wadleys Road lies to the north of Solihull station in an area known as World's End. It is a short cul-de-sac, running from the main Warwick Road to the railway. A footbridge, often used by Michael, connects it with houses on the other side of the line. Here two of the original Swindon Inter-City three-car diesel units were working the 8.10am Birmingham Snow Hill-Carmarthen on Friday 19th June 1959. The Inter-City DMUs were introduced on the Snow Hill-Gloucester-South Wales service on 17th June 1957, running via Hatton North Junction on weekdays to avoid interfering with the interval suburban service on the North Warwickshire Line. The first stop was at Stratford-upon-Avon and the DMUs took 2½ hours to reach Cardiff compared to two hours today.

On Friday 19th June 1959 5101 Class 2-6-2T 4155 passes Wadleys Road on the Down Relief line with the 8.4am Lapworth-Birmingham Snow Hill. Six non-corridor coaches were the usual formation for a peak-hour suburban train on this route. After nationalisation in 1948 the original GWR green livery of these 2-6-2Ts was replaced by unlined black, but in the late 1950s many of them received lined green livery but 4155 was not one of them. It was allocated to Worcester when built in 1947 and was transferred from Wellington to Tyseley in May 1955 and was withdrawn from that shed in September 1965.

Hawksworth Class 94xx 0-6-0PT 9432 at Wadleys Road working a short Down pick-up freight on Friday 19th June 1959. These engines were intended as a modernised version of the Collett Class 57xx panniers, with a Swindon No.10 standard taper boiler, as fitted to the 2251 Class 0-6-0s and Hawksworth's 15xx Class panniers. 210 were built but only the first ten by the GWR and the remainder by outside contractors for BR. 9432 was one of a batch of 50 built by Robert Stephenson and Hawthorn and Company in 1950-51. It was only ever allocated to Tyseley and had a very short life from new in November 1950 until withdrawn in November 1959, less than three years after the last of the class, 3409, entered service. 29 of them were withdrawn during 1959, some only seven years old.

Working bunker-first, 81xx Class 2-6-2T 8101 heads the 8.28am Solihull-Birmingham Snow Hill at Wadleys Road on Friday 19th June 1959. The ten-strong class had a complex history. The prototype Churchward Large Prairie was 99 (built 1903); in 1905-06 Nos. 3111-49 were built, based on 99 (which became 3100), but with long cone boilers. In 1927-29, these were rebalanced, giving a reduced axle loading, renumbered 5100 and 5111-49. In 1938 ten of these were rebuilt with 225lbs./sq. in. boiler pressure and 5ft. 6in. driving wheels (instead of 5ft. 8in.) in an attempt to improve their acceleration on suburban passenger work and renumbered 8100-09; fifty were to have been built but the order was cancelled on the outbreak of war. They were initially intended for London suburban work, but it was found that they had no real advantage over the 61xx Class, so they were spread around the system. 8101 nominally new from Swindon in March 1938, but was a rebuild of 5123 which dated from May 1905. It was a Kidderminster engine from rebuilding until withdrawn in March 1961.

Photographed from the Grange Road overbridge, which was closer to Olton station than to Solihull, 5101 Class 2-6-2T 4111 was working the 8.23am Lapworth-Birmingham Snow Hill on Friday 19th June 1959. It is painted in lined green livery and has the second BR crest on the sides of its tanks. 4111 is on the Down Main passing a DMU with the 6.38am from Wellington to Knowle & Dorridge on the Up Main. 4111 was built in 1936 and became a long-term Tyseley resident, and apart from one month at Stafford Road, remained there until withdrawal in September 1965. In the early 1950s there were around 30 Large Prairies shedded at Tyseley, primarily for the Birmingham area local services. More were based at Leamington Spa, Wolverhampton Stafford Road and Stourbridge Junction and thus also contributed to the operation of the area's suburban services.

We return to Solihull station, where 5101 Class 2-6-2T 4175 in grubby unlined black livery was departing from platform 4 on the Down Relief line with the 8.28am to Birmingham Snow Hill on Saturday 20th June 1959. Like 8101 the previous day on the same train (see page 30), it was a Kidderminster resident and the 8.28am Solihull-Snow Hill seems to have been a regular turn for the 2-6-2Ts shedded there. 4175 was allocated to Kidderminster from new in November 1949 until September 1964, except for three months at Gloucester in early 1958. The leading coach W6440W, in the darker BR maroon livery used on main line stock rather than the lighter red used for suburban stock, is a Diagram E.141 Composite built in 1931 for the GWR Birmingham suburban services. The signal is a typical example of ex-GWR lower-quadrant design.

This was Michael's first visit to the West Coast Main Line to take colour pictures and he was positioned on a footbridge over the ex-LNWR line, just under half a mile to the east of Tamworth station. Stanier Jubilee 4-6-0 45669 *Fisher* was approaching at speed with the 8.30am Liverpool Lime Street-Euston on Sunday 21st June 1959. The arrangement of this four-line section was, from left to right, Down Slow, Down Fast, Up Fast, Up Slow. The tower of St. Editha's church is on the extreme left and in the distance, Tamworth station is just about visible. This scene is unrecognisable now following electrification of the WCML and housing developments although the buildings behind the train remain. 45669 was one of the Jubilees named after admirals, in this case, Sir John Fisher (1841-1920). At this date it was allocated to Camden shed but was transferred to Willesden in October 1959.

The overbridge carrying Streetsbrook Road over the Snow Hill-Paddington line just to the north of Solihull station was one of Michael's favourite viewpoints. This excellent panning shot of 6001 *King Edward VII*, with the 7.25am Wolverhampton Low Level-Paddington on Wednesday 24th June 1959, with its blurred background, gives a real sense of speed. To obtain this side-on view, Michael must have positioned himself on the pavement where the road climbs to the bridge from the west. Originally allocated to Old Oak Common, 6001 was a Stafford Road engine from October 1954 until withdrawal in September 1962, and was the third King to be fitted with a double chimney, in February 1956.

Hall 4-6-0 5930 *Hannington Hall* passes through Acocks Green and South Yardley station with the 10.0am Paddington-Wolverhampton Low Level via Oxford on Saturday 4th July 1959. Until 1910 all Paddington-Birmingham trains had to run via Reading and Oxford. In that year, the GWR opened its cut-off via High Wycombe and Bicester, part of which was jointly owned with the Great Central Railway. This shortened the route by 18¾ miles, but some trains continued to use the old route, mainly to serve intermediate stations. The 10.0am from Paddington took a leisurely 3 hours 24 minutes to reach Snow Hill compared with the two-hour schedule of the expresses using the cut-off. 5930 was allocated to Banbury from April 1959 until moving to Stourbridge Junction in April 1960; it was withdrawn in September 1962.

A brand new three-car Gloucester Railway Carriage & Wagon Co. Cross-Country DMU (later Class 119) with Driving Motor Second W51099 leading, leaves Acocks Green and South Yardley station with the 1.20pm Birmingham Moor Street-Leamington Spa on Saturday 4th July 1959. Tyseley depot received two of these units in July 1959, with another one following in October and a further five were transferred from Cardiff in July 1962. They were built on longer 64ft. 6in. underframes than the suburban 57ft. 6in. units and included a buffet car; they were painted in multiple-unit malachite green, lined because they were intended for longer-distance operation, with 'speed whiskers' and white cab domes. Although, as the name suggests, intended for longer journeys than this, they were quite frequently used for local services on filling-in turns. The station name board in the background, with its crudely painted "AND" replacing the applied wooden letters which had fallen off, was by this time quite a well-known feature of this station. The benches below it feature the GWR monogram. When opened in 1852 the station was named Acocks Green but in 1878 it was renamed Acocks Green and South Yardley to attract the growing commuter traffic to Birmingham. The station reverted to its original shorter name on 6th May 1968.

King Class 4-6-0 6009 *King Charles II* is about to enter the gloom of Snow Hill tunnel as it leaves platform 7 at Birmingham Snow Hill with the Up "Cambrian Coast Express" on Saturday 4th July 1959. 6009 was an Old Oak Common engine from new in March 1928 until withdrawal in September 1962. Although Wolverhampton and Shrewsbury were less than twenty rail miles apart, the Kings were prohibited from working between those two points because of restrictions over Shifnal viaduct. In 1953 it was reconstructed enabling them to work through to Shrewsbury, although such instances remained sporadic, and the Kings were not used regularly north of Wolverhampton until 1959. As from 20th April, they took over the "Cambrian Coast Express" diagram between Paddington and Shrewsbury formerly worked by Castles, although this soon ended when Castles returned in late August.

Another picture of Kidderminster's 5101 Class 2-6-2T 4175 departing Solihull station with the 8.28am to Snow Hill, a journey of just 21 minutes, on Saturday 4th July 1959. It is leaving from a different platform, on the Down Main, than two weeks earlier (page 32) and the first coach is a BR 1951-built Diagram C.83 Hawksworth designed non-corridor Second which is in the lighter BR crimson suburban livery. These had longer underframes than the pre-war suburban stock (63ft. 0¾in. compared with 61ft. 2in.) and could accommodate a hundred passengers; note also the deeper windows. The West Midlands area was the last on the Western Region to have regular steam loco-hauled suburban services, but the non-corridor stock was replaced in 1962. The leading coach appears to be empty whereas a few years before it would have been packed with office staff who had to work Saturday mornings, but that practice was dying out by this time.

Hatton is the last station before Warwick on the Snow Hill-Paddington line and is closer to the village of Shrewley than to Hatton itself. A triangular junction gives access to the original line to Stratford, the importance of which was reduced after the opening of the North Warwickshire line in 1907-08. Castle 4-6-0 5047 *Earl of Dartmouth* approaches the junction and station with an excursion, probably originating at Wolverhampton Low Level, bound for Weymouth on Sunday 5th July 1959. 5047, here looking rather grubby, was one of the engines given the names of earls which had been removed from the Dukedog 4-4-0s, in this case from 3204. 5047 was built in April 1936 as *Compton Castle* and renamed in August 1937. It was allocated to Wolverhampton Stafford Road from November 1954 until withdrawal in September 1962. It had a straight sided Hawksworth tender from February 1953 until December 1960.

Photographed from the footbridge, 7026 *Tenby Castle* with the 6.40pm Wolverhampton Low Level-Paddington passes over the level crossing at Bentley Heath on Sunday 5th July 1959. It was built by British Railways, entering service in August 1949, and was allocated to Stafford Road until the shed closed in 1963. The original Hawksworth tender had been replaced by an earlier Collett type in January 1957. The Knowle & Dorridge North Goods Yard and Shed, just visible in the right distance, were built in 1932 during the quadrupling of the line to replace the original goods facilities at the south end of that station.

Looking towards Coventry from the overbridge at Stechford station on the former LNWR line into Birmingham from the south, Stanier 8F 2-8-0 48389, having finished its shunting, was propelling its train into the station on Monday 6th July 1959. After taking on water, it will return to the head of the train and depart via the freight-only line to Aston on the Grand Junction route to the north.

Until November 1960, 48389 was allocated to Longsight, the principal ex-LMS shed in Manchester, and it is likely that it was heading back to Lancashire. Note the shunter with his pole, used for coupling and un-coupling loose-coupled wagons.

Stechford No.1 signal box controlled the layout here and the nine-road Down Yard (opposite) which is mostly out of sight in this picture. The factory to the left is that of Parkinson Cowan who manufactured gas cookers here there until 1995 and the presence of an open wagon shows that it was still rail-served at this date.

Tyseley 5101 class 2-6-2T 4155, in unlined black livery, arrives at Acocks Green and South Yardley station with the 6.25pm Knowle & Dorridge-Birmingham Moor Street on Monday 6th July 1959. 4155, on the Down Relief line and hauling the usual six non-corridor coaches, was working bunker-first, which was normal practice for Down trains. The line on the extreme right is the Down goods loop. In the distance, an express train is approaching at speed on the Down Main and was probably the 4.10pm from Paddington, due to pass Tyseley at 6.37pm. The local train was due to depart Acocks Green at 6.38pm which suggests the 4.10pm is close to right time, perhaps no more than two minutes behind schedule. On the extreme left edge of the photograph is the chimney of the Rover armaments factory which was built in 1937.

An unidentified Castle Class 4-6-0 with a Hawksworth tender, working northbound with "The Cornishman" approaching Acocks Green and South Yardley station on Monday 6th July 1959. This was the 10.30am from Penzance to Wolverhampton Low Level which also conveyed a portion from Kingswear. The combination of a train reporting number and headboard sometimes made identifying locomotives difficult, especially if the cabside number plate was dirty. In GWR days, the numbers were painted on the buffer beam. The BR Mark 1 coaches are painted in a version of the former GWR 'chocolate and cream' livery, introduced by the Western Region for its named trains in 1957. The 33-lever Acocks Green signal box was opened in 1907, replacing an earlier one; it closed in September 1969.

Stanier Class 5 4-6-0 45269 approaches Acocks Green and South Yardley station on the Down Main with a short Class D fitted freight on Monday 6th July 1959. 45269 was shedded at Saltley, the former Midland Railway's principal depot in Birmingham and will probably access London Midland Region metals at Bordesley Junction and continue to Washwood Heath Sidings. People living in Roberts Road had a good view of passing trains from their front bedroom windows, although it must have been rather noisy!

At this date, a BR Standard Class 5 4-6-0 was a rare sight on the Western Region in the Birmingham area, although they were common enough on the LMR lines through New Street. Here 73096 works the 3.18pm Paddington-Wolverhampton Low Level through Solihull station on Monday 6th July 1959. The 3.18pm ran via Oxford and with many stops took 4½ hours to reach Snow Hill, being overtaken by both the 4.10pm and 5.10pm from Paddington running via Bicester. This was a train which could normally be relied on to produce an ex-GWR 4-6-0. 73096 is paired with a BR1C high-sided 9 ton, 4,725 gallon tender, which had increased coal and water capacity. Visually, these could easily be distinguished from the smaller BR1 tender of the original members of the class which had inset bunkers. Originally at Patricroft from new in November 1955, 73096 was transferred to Shrewsbury in August 1958. This picture illustrates the standard station layout of most of the stations on this four-track stretch of line. There were two wide island platforms, with their deeply canopied buildings. The train is on the Down Main, as one would expect. The Up Main is behind the station name board with the Up Relief in the foreground and the Down Relief on the right of the picture.

King Class 4-6-0 6001 *King Edward VII* passing through Widney Manor station on the Up Main line with the 7.25am Wolverhampton-Paddington on Wednesday 8th July 1959. At this time, it was common Western Region practice for a locomotive to be allocated to a particular turn for several weeks, or even months. We saw 6001, a Wolverhampton Stafford Road engine, working the same train at Solihull two weeks earlier, on 24th June (see page 34). This was a popular train with businessmen travelling to the Capital. The layout at Widney Manor differed from the stations between Bordesley and Solihull which were all two island platform layouts with similar buildings.

Class 5101 2-6-2T 4103 departs from Widney Manor station with a train bound for Knowle & Dorridge on Wednesday 8th July 1959. This was an unusual working which originated at Acocks Green, leaving there at 7.54am. From Knowle & Dorridge the train continued as empty stock to Lapworth (arriving at 8.14am), returning as the busy 8.33am Lapworth to Snow Hill. The 2-6-2T was working bunker-first, whereas the normal practice was for tank engines on Up trains to travel chimney-first. 4103 was allocated to Leamington Spa between November 1957 and August 1959 and is in lined green livery, although it has the original BR 'cycling lion' emblem. The lineside looks parched, just waiting for a spark from an engine to set it alight.

A three-car Derby-built suburban DMU approaches Acocks Green and South Yardley with the 1.20pm from Birmingham Moor Street to Leamington Spa on Wednesday 8th July 1959. This photograph was taken opposite the station entrance on the road bridge in Sherbourne Road, part of the A4040 Birmingham Outer Ring Road, the route of the Outer Circle 11 bus route (for many years the longest urban bus route in Europe, covering 27 miles and with 233 stops counting in both directions). It has and remains a popular viewpoint although now of just two tracks. There is evidence of a lineside fire, a regular hazard during steam days in dry summer months, which must have been of some concern to the long-established firm of motor engineers nearby, whose business is still in existence today.

A six-car rake of two Swindon Inter-City units, forming the 8.10am Birmingham Snow Hill-Carmarthen, passes through Widney Manor station on Thursday 9th July 1959. The very uninspiring front end of the leading driving motor brake second (with a luggage space) had an 'intermediate' half-cab with central gangway connection that allowed through access to all vehicles when two three-car units were coupled as a six-car set. Note the speed 'whiskers' and lining continued across the corridor cover and the unusual letter 'A' headcodes on backlit stencilled metal sheets. The six three-car units were built on 64ft. 6in. underframes compared with 57ft. 6in. for the suburban DMUs and comprised twelve power cars, two trailer buffet firsts (the second vehicle in this photograph) and four trailer cars; four of the units were maintained at Tyseley. Their stay in the West Midlands was about to end as in the late summer of 1959; they were replaced by Swindon-built Cross-Country units (later Class 120) and the Inter-City units transferred to Scotland for the Edinburgh-Glasgow service, joining similar units which were later designated Class 126.

An uncommon sight in the West Midlands, Class 72xx 2-8-2T 7237 approaches the Woodcock Lane overbridge to the south of Acocks Green and South Yardley station with an Up coal train on Friday 10th July 1959. These engines were Collett rebuilds of the Churchward Class 42xx 2-8-0T and 7237 was rebuilt from 5272 in early 1936. The larger coal bunker of the rebuilt engines certainly gave them a greater range, but another reason for the rebuilds was to create work, financed in part by government loans, during the Great Depression of the 1930s. The original engines rarely left South Wales but, while most of the rebuilds were also based there, they could and did range more widely. In 1958 just four out of the 72xx class of 54 were allocated outside South Wales.

Having previously been at Leamington Spa from January 1948 until September 1952, 7237 returned when it was transferred to Banbury shortly before this photograph was taken having spent six months out of use in store, probably at Severn Tunnel Junction. However, it soon went back to South Wales, moving to Aberdare in September 1959.

British Railways Standard Class 4 2-6-4T 80081 arrives at Stechford station with the 12.42 Coventry-Birmingham New Street on Wednesday 15th July 1959. Local trains on this line which were still steam-worked were usually in the hands of a Stanier or Fairburn 2-6-4Ts, or an Ivatt Class 2 2-6-0. Although 80081 is rather grimy, its coaches are in immaculate condition. 80081 was allocated to Bletchley from new in April 1954 until November 1959, but was transferred to the Southern Region at Stewarts Lane the following month. A railwayman is striding purposefully towards the photographer. Perhaps he was going to "have a word". The station staff on this route were not always particularly welcoming to enthusiasts, but, no doubt, Michael would have had official permission to be there. Above the rear of the train is the station entrance building on Station Road. This was re-sited in Victoria Road when the station was completely rebuilt when the line was electrified in the 1960s. The one-time timber yard to the left owned by local firm Cartwrights was still rail-served at this date.

A typically grimy Stanier Class 5 4-6-0, 44716 from Rugby shed, awaits departure from Birmingham New Street's platform 3 with the 3.55pm to Norwich on Saturday 18th July 1959. The train will travel via the now-closed ex-LNWR line from Rugby via Market Harborough and Seaton Junction. This train was the return working of a service which left Norwich at 7.50am, reaching New Street at 12.50pm. BR's carmine and cream (aka 'blood and custard') livery did not really suit Gresley teak coaches, as can be seen from the leading brake second. The soot-encrusted brick building rising above the platform canopy is the Odeon cinema in New Street.

A smartly dressed spotter consults his ABC as Stanier Class 5 4-6-0 45071, quite respectably turned out by the nearby Monument Lane shed, stands at Birmingham New Street's platform 6 with the 10.45am Hastings-Walsall on Saturday 18th July 1959. The train would have travelled from the Southern Region to Willesden Junction via the West London line, a route followed by the joint LNWR and London, Brighton and South Coast Railway "Sunny South Express" before the Great War. Most trains to Walsall from New Street take the old Grand Junction line through Aston and Perry Barr but because this train has come in from the south, this one will gain that route via Soho South and Perry Barr North Junctions. The large building rising above the station is the Queens Hotel, the less than beautiful rear of which had been exposed to public gaze by the demolition of the badly war-damaged station overall roof in the early 1940s. Residents would have had full benefit of the sights, sounds, smoke and steam from the station!

Jubilee 4-6-0 45592 *Indore* arrives at Birmingham New Street's platform 3 with the 4.0pm Wolverhampton High Level-Euston on Saturday 18th July 1959. This was the longest platform on the North Western side of New Street and was used by most London departures. A group of spotters are at the end of the platform, not a particularly good vantage point because they could not see the activity on the Midland side of the station. Perhaps they had been 'moved on' from the east end of platform 6, the best spot, by the British Transport Police. A DMU is standing at either platform 1 or 2, which were known as the South Staffordshire bays. On the right is the No.1 signal box which controlled movements from the eastern end of the North Western side of the station. 45592 was on loan to Bushbury from Camden where it had been allocated since June 1953.

Hatton Bank is where the Paddington-Snow Hill line climbs out of the Avon valley onto the West Midlands plateau. It begins just before Warwick station and continues for seven miles, mainly at 1 in 103 or 1 in 110, to a point just beyond Hatton North Junction. The Down goods loop on the right of the train allowed goods trains moving slowly up the gradient to be passed by passenger services, and banking engines were usually available at Warwick. The line here is closely paralleled by the Grand Union Canal, which makes the same climb by means of a flight of twenty-one locks. Michael took a number of photographs near the summit. Here, what appears to be an unusual case of a 2-8-0 on a passenger train was actually a Down empty carriage working, headed by 3856 from Banbury shed passing under Dark Lane bridge near the top of the bank on Saturday 18th July 1959. It was one of the later Collett 2884 class 2-8-0s, which were a modernised version of the Churchward 28xx class. They could be distinguished from the original engines by their side-window cabs and outside steam pipes. Built in 1942, 3856 was transferred from Banbury depot to Severn Tunnel Junction in December 1959 from where it was withdrawn in October 1964.

The Gloucester Railway Carriage and Wagon Company's single-car diesel units (Class 122 under TOPS), introduced in 1958, were known to enthusiasts as 'Bubble Cars'. They were really intended for use on branch lines, but some were employed on lightly loaded suburban services in the West Midlands. Here, we have two for the price of one, working the 6.45pm Leamington Spa to Stratford-on-Avon near the summit of Hatton Bank on Saturday 18th July 1959. The train will travel via Hatton Station Junction and Hatton West Junction.

An Old Oak Common engine since March 1958, Hall class 4-6-0 5923 *Colston Hall* nears the summit of Hatton Bank with the 3.18pm Paddington-Wolverhampton Low Level via Oxford on Saturday 18th July 1959. 5923 was one of a number of the class which were not given the names of stately homes, in this case that of a concert venue in Bristol. It was opened in 1867 and named after Edward Colston who, as well as being a benefactor to the people of Bristol, was also heavily involved in the trans-Atlantic slave trade. The decision to rename the concert hall was taken in 2017 and brought forward in 2020 after the anti-racism protests of that summer, when Colston's statue was pitched into Bristol harbour. The hall is now known as the Bristol Beacon. Of course, none of this affected 5923, which was scrapped in 1963.

A 'going away shot' of a three-car Derby suburban DMU on the 6.25pm Birmingham Moor Street-Leamington Spa going downhill at the bridge near the top of Hatton Bank on Saturday 18th July 1959. Judging by the parched appearance of the cutting sides in these pictures, there must have been a recent period of dry weather.

The 6.25pm Knowle & Dorridge-Birmingham Moor Street seems to have been one of Michael's favourites, probably because it could be relied upon to produce steam at this date. Here it was arriving at Acocks Green and South Yardley station on Monday 20th July 1959, taken from the same location as the picture of 4155 photographed two weeks earlier (see page 42). The engine running bunker-first was green liveried 6105, one of a class normally associated with suburban services out of Paddington. It was one of the six Collett 61xx 2-6-2Ts transferred to Tyseley in October 1953 as replacements for the Standard 82xxx 2-6-2Ts. It left in April 1955 for a few weeks at Neyland in south west Wales and on its return remained at Tyseley until November 1959 when it moved to Didcot.

Castle class 5058 *Earl of Clancarty* with pilot engine 2251 class 0-6-0 2211 approach Acocks Green and South Yardley on Monday 20th July 1959 with "The Cornishman", the 10.30am Penzance-Wolverhampton Low Level which included through coaches from Kingswear that were combined with the main train at Exeter St. Davids. The assisting engine had been added at Stratford-upon-Avon for the bank to Wilmcote which rose to 1 in 75 and in accordance with normal GWR/Western Region practice the pilot engine was positioned behind the train engine. 2211 had been transferred to Tyseley the previous month and would have been based at the sub-shed at Stratford for pilot duties. 5058, allocated to Plymouth's Laira shed between March 1950 and September 1961, was originally named *Newport Castle* when built in May 1937. This was short-lived and in September 1937 it received one of the Earl names that was planned for Dukedog 4-4-0 3215 but never carried by that engine.

A gleaming King Class 4-6-0 approaches Acocks Green and South Yardley station with the 5.10pm Paddington-Wolverhampton Low Level on Monday 20th July 1959. 6022 *King Edward III* had just been transferred from Old Oak Common to Stafford Road on 18th June. The Mark 1 coaching stock, in a mixture of the early British Railways 'blood and custard' and the later maroon liveries, is typical of the period.

The 3.18pm Paddington-Wolverhampton Low Level via Oxford passes through Solihull behind Worcester's 4088 *Dartmouth Castle* on Monday 20th July 1959, two weeks after the picture on page 45 of 73096 working the same train. Built in July 1925, and fitted with a double chimney in May 1958, 4088 was looking rather woebegone as someone had attempted to make it look more presentable by painting the smokebox door numbers white. 4088 went into Swindon Works for a Heavy General overhaul four weeks after this photograph was taken and would remain in service for another five years. The 3.18pm, calling at many intermediate stations, regularly included vehicles which could not be conveyed on the two-hour expresses to the West Midlands, in this case a horsebox followed by a GWR Fruit D van.

Two three-car Derby-built suburban DMUs on the 7.30am Leamington Spa-Wellington arrive at Widney Manor station on Monday 27th July 1959. This service waited at Birmingham Snow Hill's platform 1 from 8.17am to 8.35am where it was overtaken by the 7.45am Leamington Spa to Birkenhead Woodside which was due at platform 5 from 8.29am to 8.32am. The curious contraption on a tripod to the right of the train which incorporates a windmill was an anemometer to measure wind speed.

Running on the Up Relief line, a three-car Derby built suburban DMU arrives at Solihull station with the 11.0am Wellington-Leamington Spa on Sunday 2nd August 1959. On the right, the goods yard seems to be doing business with several coal wagons, including three BR steel-bodied mineral wagons, and an earlier wooden-bodied example and behind them a number of vans. Goods facilities at Solihull were withdrawn in July 1964 and the layout now is a basic two-track railway. In the distance is Michael's frequent vantage point, Streetsbrook Road overbridge.

Photographed from the overbridge at Shirley station on the North Warwickshire line from Stratford-on-Avon to Tyseley and Birmingham, a three-car Swindon-built Cross-Country DMU (Class 120 under TOPS) passes the new housing estate as it arrives with the 5.30pm Stratford-on-Avon to Birmingham Snow Hill on Saturday 8th August 1959. The early units were allocated to Cardiff Canton with several going to Tyseley between March and June 1958. When first introduced, they were used on services between Cardiff and Bristol and between Birmingham Snow Hill and South Wales via Stratford and soon after between Birmingham Snow Hill and Oxford. As more units were delivered, they were used more widely on other services to and from the West Midlands and were regularly used on local services as fill-in duties. When built, the centre cars were trailer second buffets reflecting the employment of the units on long-distance services, but these were withdrawn at the start of the winter 1958 timetable. On the unit in this picture the buffet car had been replaced by trailer from a three-car suburban unit, hence the absence of the cream lining along the bodyside on the outer vehicles.

Knowle & Dorridge is on the Birmingham Snow Hill-Leamington Spa line, between Widney Manor and Lapworth. Some suburban trains terminated there, as they still do. Today it is called simply Dorridge, since it is closer to that village than to Knowle, although the two places now form a continuous built-up area, popular with commuters. A travel-stained BR-built Castle 4-6-0 7026 *Tenby Castle* was passing through the station with the 12.15pm Kingswear-Wolverhampton Low Level, identified by the chalked 851 reporting number, on Friday 14th August 1959. 7026, new in August 1949, spent almost its whole working life allocated to Wolverhampton Stafford Road, only moving to Tyseley in July 1964 prior to withdrawal in October 1964.

Class 5101 2-6-2T 4126 passes through Knowle & Dorridge station with an Up freight on Friday 14th August 1959. The larger GWR 2-6-2Ts based at Tyseley and other local depots were primarily used on suburban passenger workings out of Snow Hill and Moor Street until displaced by diesel multiple units from 1957 onwards, but they were also useful performers on local freight workings especially once they were no longer required for passenger operations. The engine is in plain black livery with the first BR emblem. By this time, some of the class had acquired lined green livery, usually with the later BR crest, when they were repainted at Swindon after a Heavy General overhaul. 4126 was allocated to Tyseley from December 1958 until it became an early withdrawal in April 1962. The bridge in the background carried a public footpath and has since been replaced by a modern version.

Stafford Road's 6005 *King George II* was slowing, probably for a signal check, as it passed Knowle & Dorridge station on Friday 14th August 1959. The train was the 5.10pm Paddington-Wolverhampton Low Level, the heaviest express of the day loaded to thirteen coaches and a popular train for businessmen returning from the Capital. Knowle & Dorridge enjoyed a single fast through train to Paddington at 8.14am and the 5.10pm from Paddington called in the Down direction but, until the introduction of the Birmingham Pullman in 1960, Solihull itself had no regular express service to or from London.

The passengers on the Down Main platform at Knowle & Dorridge were awaiting the arrival of the 7.45am Leamington Spa to Birkenhead Woodside (shown in the next photograph) as BR Standard Class 5 4-6-0 73029 rushes through whilst working the 7.50am Birmingham Snow Hill-Weymouth on Saturday 15th August 1959. For many years there had been a daily through service from Wolverhampton and Birmingham to Weymouth but by 1959 the service was reduced to Saturdays Only, albeit with a second train leaving Birmingham ten minutes later (page 71). 73029 was a Weymouth engine from September 1958 until August 1964. Knowle & Dorridge was one of the stations with three platforms, the two outer ones (Up Main which this train is passing) and Down Relief, having a single face; in between there was an island platform (Down Main and Up Relief). Other stations on the line (e.g. Acocks Green and South Yardley or Solihull, see page 45) had two island platforms.

43xx Class 2-6-0 6391 arrives at Knowle & Dorridge with the 7.45am Leamington Spa-Birkenhead Woodside on Saturday 15th August 1959 which was scheduled to reach Birkenhead at 11.43am. The city gents on the Down Main platform are indicative that stockbroker's offices and banks in those days still opened for business on Saturdays. The 1921-built 6391 had a peripatetic existence and was allocated to Swindon at the date of this photograph.

Instantly recognisable from the earlier Halls because of its plate-framed leading bogie and modified front frames, Hawksworth Modified Hall 4-6-0 6967 *Willesley Hall* roars through Knowle & Dorridge station with the 8.0am Birmingham Snow Hill-Weymouth on Saturday 15th August 1959. For many years there had been a daily through service from Wolverhampton and Birmingham to Weymouth. Leaving Weymouth Town the train continued to the Quay with passengers for the Channel Island steamer. The return left the Quay at 4.5pm and reached Snow Hill at 9.51pm, a long day for passengers whose steamer had sailed from Jersey at 8.0am! A Southall locomotive from October 1958 until moving to Oxford in November 1963, 6967 was one of the last ex-GWR locomotives in service and was withdrawn at the end of 1965.

With the houses of Bryanston Road in the background on Sunday 16th August 1959, a lovely summer morning, a three-car Derby-built suburban DMU was working the 9.20am Birmingham Moor Street-Leamington Spa on the Up Relief line about halfway between Olton and Solihull. The signal post situated in the 'six foot' between the Down Main and the Up Relief is an indication that this route was built to Brunel's broad gauge (7ft. 0¼in.). The two outer tracks were added when the line was quadrupled in1932-33.

A three-car Derby-built suburban DMU had just left Hall Green on the North Warwickshire line with the 8.15am Stratford-Birmingham Snow Hill and was about to pass under the York Road overbridge south of Spring Road station on Sunday 16th August 1959.

The North Warwickshire line, opened in 1907/08 from Tyseley to Bearley West Junction, not only opened up the south western suburbs of Birmingham for future commuter traffic and shortened the distance to Stratford, but it also produced a direct route for the GWR between Birmingham, Bristol and South Wales. The stations on the line were close together, in an attempt to win back suburban traffic lost to trams and buses, so the DMU would already be slowing for the Spring Road stop. Hall Green Goods Yard on the right was closed in May 1968.

This picture was taken from the north or 'country end' of Widney Manor station as 6008 *King James II* approaches at speed with an excursion from Wolverhampton Low Level to Paddington on Sunday 16th August 1959. 6008 was allocated to Stafford Road from 1930 until 1952 when it was transferred to Plymouth Laira but had returned to the Wolverhampton shed in February 1959. It had been fitted with a double blastpipe and chimney and replacement front frames and inside cylinder block in July 1957. The goods shed on the right appears to be derelict, although in the distance there are some wagons parked on the siding. Goods facilities were eventually withdrawn in May 1963 and the site is now occupied by housing.

A three-car Derby-built suburban DMU on the 10.00am Wellington-Leamington Spa arrives at Lapworth station on Sunday 16th August 1959. This is one of the second batch of these units with the two-aspect train reporting code box replacing the centre lamp of the earlier units; the reporting boxes were rarely used in practice. Lapworth, at the end of the four-track section of the main line from Birmingham, was the southern terminating point for many of the Birmingham local services, although some workings continued to Leamington Spa. From the line's opening in 1854 until 1902 the station was known as Kingswood. In the distance is the Chapel Lane overbridge, one of Michael's favourite photographic locations.

6022 *King Edward III* approaches Lapworth station with the 8.5am Birkenhead Woodside-Paddington on Sunday 16th August 1959 which was scheduled to arrive in London at 2.20pm, taking 48 minutes longer than the corresponding weekday train which left Birkenhead at 8.55am. 6022 which was a Stafford Road engine would have taken over this train at Wolverhampton Low Level. In the distance, 43xx 2-6-0 6317 was shunting in the goods yard.

Two three-car Derby-built suburban DMUs forming the 5.52pm Birmingham Snow Hill-Lapworth (the 4.25pm ex-Wellington) were approaching Bentley Heath level crossing on the Up Relief line on Monday 17th August 1959. Bentley Heath, which had no station, is between Widney Manor and Knowle & Dorridge. The setting is not so rural today, because there has been a considerable amount of housing development in the area, and the M42 motorway passes under the railway between here and Widney Manor, the distant signals for which are in the background on the left.

One of Michael's favourite locations on the Snow Hill-Paddington line was at the Hillfield Road 'underbridge' half a mile south of Widney Manor station, surrounded by delightful countryside, a remnant of the ancient Forest of Arden. Today the 'underbridge' is just a little-used footpath. 6022 *King Edward III* was about to cross the bridge with the 5.10pm Paddington-Wolverhampton Low Level on Monday 17th August 1959. It had been transferred from Old Oak Common to Wolverhampton Stafford Road in June 1959.

Pontypool Road Grange 4-6-0 6819 *Highnam Grange* with the 7.45am Leamington Spa-Birkenhead Woodside was starting away from Solihull station, towards Streetsbrook Road bridge on Tuesday 18th August 1959. The Granges were built between 1936 and 1939 using the wheels and motion from withdrawn Class 43xx 2-6-0s. They were classic mixed traffic engines and, although their driving wheels were 4 inches smaller, some enginemen considered that they had a greater turn of speed than the Halls. They could be distinguished from the Halls by the running plate raised over the cylinders. The leading coach W5456 is a Collett D115 60ft. brake third dating from 1932. The tracks nearest to the camera are part of Solihull goods depot which closed in July 1964.

Stechford was (and is) an important junction, where the line to Aston diverges from the main line, giving access to the original Grand Junction route to Stafford, Crewe and the north and providing a means by which freight trains passing through the city could avoid New Street. It was also used as part of a diversionary route when there was engineering work on the West Coast Main Line through Nuneaton, Tamworth and Lichfield. A Hughes-Fowler Crab 2-6-0 42814 was about to take the Aston line, which curves away to the right, with a freight on Tuesday 18th August 1959; the main line heading to New Street can be glimpsed at the extreme left. 42814 was allocated to Longsight shed, Manchester, from February 1949 until November 1960 and it is likely that this train is bound for the north west.

Acocks Green and South Yardley saw a considerable amount of Birmingham commuter traffic. 5101 Class 2-6-2T 4118 was arriving at the Down Main platform with the 5.35pm Birmingham Snow Hill-Lapworth on Tuesday 18th August 1959. In those days, suburban trains had First Class accommodation as shown by the leading coach, a 60ft. composite built at Swindon for the LMR in the early 1950s to a slightly modified GWR 1937-40 design. 4118 was allocated to Tyseley from new in 1936 until 1946 and returned to the West Midlands in September 1954 at Leamington Spa, remaining there until withdrawal in September 1962. The seat in front of the large GWR running-in board was much used by trainspotters, who were always tolerated by the station staff. Today the station is called simply Acocks Green.

Green-liveried 61xx 2-6-2T 6105 on the 6.25pm Knowle & Dorridge-Birmingham Moor Street is arriving at Widney Manor station on Tuesday 18th August 1959. 6105 was one of the six 61xx Class transferred from the London area to Tyseley in 1953 as replacements for new standard 82xxx 2-6-2Ts which had been found unsuitable for the demanding Birmingham suburban services. It left in April 1955 for a few weeks at Neyland in south west Wales and on its return remained at Tyseley until November 1959 when it moved to Didcot.

Wolverhampton Stafford Road's 6008 *King James II*, running on the Up Main line, approaches Widney Manor station on Tuesday 18th August 1959 with the 4.10pm Paddington-Birkenhead Woodside which it would take through to Wolverhampton. 6008 had been transferred to Wolverhampton Stafford Road from Laira shed at Plymouth in February 1959 following the arrival there of the Warship diesel-hydraulics. The two white notices on either platform with a figure 6 indicate to DMU drivers where to stop with a 6-car train. The DMUs used on this line were three-car units, running with two sets together at peak times. For many years, drivers of steam locomotives had known where to stop without the aid of a sign!

For most of the year, the 12.15pm from Kingswear to Wolverhampton Low Level formed a portion of "The Cornishman" from Penzance and was attached to the main train at Exeter St. Davids but, during the peak summer season between 24th July and 21st August the trains ran separately, approximately 15 minutes apart. On Tuesday 18th August 1959, headed by Castle 4-6-0 5070 *Sir Daniel Gooch*, the Kingswear train was approaching Widney Manor although it was timetabled to use the North Warwickshire line between Stratford and Tyseley; it was scheduled to reach Wolverhampton Low Level at 7.25pm. 5070 was allocated to Wolverhampton Stafford Road from 1940 until February 1960 when it was transferred to Shrewsbury. Note the reversed "Cornishman" headboard and the full consist of BR Mark 1 coaches in the 'chocolate and cream' livery used by the Western Region from 1957 for its named trains.

Fowler Class 4F 0-6-0 43924 heads a Class D fitted freight north at Widney Manor on 18th August 1959. At this time, the engine was allocated to Gloucester Barnwood shed, and would have regularly worked to the Birmingham area. The Midland Railway built 192 of these locomotives from 1911, with the LMS adding a further 580 between 1924 and 1941. Built in October 1920, 43924 was withdrawn from Bristol Barrow Road shed in 1965 and moved to Woodhams Bros. scrapyard at Barry Docks. In 1968 it was bought for preservation by the Keighley & Worth Valley Railway, becoming the first of 213 locomotives to be rescued from Barry. Although four 4Fs are preserved, 43924 is the only Midland Railway-built example. It has appeared in several films including 'Testament of Youth' and 'Swallows & Amazons' and in 2021 had a starring role in the 'The Railway Children Return'.

On Tuesday 18th August 1959, two three-car Derby-built suburban units forming the 6.48pm Lapworth-Wellington approach Widney Manor station. The 'second man' in the cab has noticed the photographer. Double-manning of these units was not common – perhaps this man was learning the route or simply hitching a ride home. The destination indicator reads Birmingham Snow Hill where there was a 16-minute layover at Snow Hill before one of the two units departed to Wellington at 7.35pm with the other going to Stratford-upon-Avon at 7.40pm.

Working tender-first at the north end of Birmingham Snow Hill station on Sunday 23rd August 1959, 4956 *Plowden Hall*, a Cardiff Canton engine from February 1959, was on the Down through road with the empty stock which it had brought in from Tyseley carriage sidings for an excursion to Weston-super-Mare, a popular resort for Brummies. After passing through the station, it will run round its train and then bring it back to one of the Up platforms before heading south through Tyseley and the North Warwickshire line to Weston. The Snow Hill north end pilot, another Hall, is standing by the North signal box, which was a curious structure, raised on steel columns, with its superstructure overhanging. It dated from the installation of electrical signalling in 1910. The North and South signal boxes were replaced in September 1960 by an entrance-exit signalling panel located in the former Third Class ladies' waiting room on platform 1/5.

Michael was standing on the Woodcock Lane overbridge just to the south of Acocks Green and South Yardley station, with the tall poplar trees, as so often, forming the background to his picture. 4087 *Cardigan Castle* was approaching with the northbound "The Cornishman" on Wednesday 26th August 1959. As one of the three titled trains which passed through Birmingham Snow Hill (the others being "The Inter-City" and "The Cambrian Coast Express") the train consisted of BR Mark 1 coaches in chocolate and cream livery whilst an attractive heraldic headboard adorns the engine. This service connected Wolverhampton with Penzance, usually running via the North Warwickshire line. 4087 was based at Plymouth Laira shed from 1941 until 1963 and a rare visitor to Birmingham. It was one of the early Castles, entering service in June 1925 and was fitted with a double chimney in February 1958.

Two three-car Derby suburban DMUs on the Up Relief line leave Widney Manor station with the 4.25pm Wellington-Lapworth on Thursday 27th August 1959. Unlike some of the other stations on this line, which had two island platforms, Widney Manor had only one island, serving the Up Relief and Down Main, with two outer platforms for the Up Main and Down Relief.

Stanier Class 5 4-6-0 44859 approaches Widney Manor station with a Down Class D fitted freight on Thursday 27th August 1959. 44859 was allocated to Saltley, the former Midland Railway shed in Birmingham. This train would probably access the London Midland Region at Bordesley Junction and is probably bound for Washwood Heath sidings. At this time, the most common ex-LMS engines seen on this ex-GWR line were 8F 2-8-0s, some of which were based at Western Region sheds, but the Black Fives were becoming a frequent sight.

This picture was taken from the Sherbourne Road overbridge at Acocks Green and South Yardley station. Castle class 4-6-0 5045 *Earl of Dudley* was approaching with the 7.20am SO Pwllheli-Paddington on Saturday 29th August 1959. 5045, built in March 1936, was originally named *Bridgwater Castle*, but was renamed in September 1937. A series of 'Earl' names had been given to Collett's Dukedog 4-4-0s, rebuilt from much older Duke and Bulldog engines. Some of the earls apparently objected to their names being associated with such antiquated looking machines, so these were transferred to a batch of Castles. The *Bridgwater Castle* name was not wasted and was used on Castle 5096 when that was built in June 1939. 5045 was allocated to Wolverhampton Stafford Road from November 1950 until withdrawal in September 1962. The signal post on the left between the Down Relief and Down Main carries the Acocks Green starter and the Tyseley distant.

Another picture taken from the Sherbourne Road overbridge at Acocks Green and South Yardley, looking towards Tyseley and Snow Hill. The entrance building, with its ticket office, was situated on this bridge and from it, stairs gave access to the two island platforms. As they approach from the Tyseley direction, the tracks can be seen fanning out to make space for the two island platforms. One of Wolverhampton Stafford Road's King 4-6-0s, 6020 *King Henry IV*, was passing with the 11.10am Paddington-Birkenhead Woodside on Saturday 29th August 1959.

Tyseley is an important junction where the North Warwickshire line to Stratford-on-Avon diverges from Paddington line. As well as carriage sidings and a large goods shed with extensive sidings, it was the location of the GWR's engine shed serving Birmingham. 5921 *Bingley Hall*, a Banbury engine since January 1958, passes through the station with the 9.15am Margate-Wolverhampton Low Level, on Saturday 29th August 1959, that also conveyed through coaches from Hastings and Sandwich. Green Southern Region coaches such as the Southern Railway Maunsell design at the front of the train were a daily sight on the Western Region through Birmingham on trains from resorts in the south of England, and particularly on summer Saturdays when between 1.57pm and 3.4pm there were no fewer than six Saturdays Only holiday express trains from the south passing through Tyseley. 5921 was not named after a stately home but an exhibition hall in Birmingham, the first purpose-built example in Great Britain, built in 1850, the year before the more famous Crystal Palace. Sadly, it was destroyed by fire in 1984.

The corridor along the railway and the Grand Union Canal through Small Heath and Tyseley was highly industrialised. Many of the factories manufactured motor vehicle components, like the Girling works owned by Lucas Industries, here in the background, which was adjacent to the Rover car works and made brake systems. The BSA (Birmingham Small Arms) factory together with that belonging to the Singer Car Company, was served by a branch from the GWR line. All this industrial activity generated considerable freight traffic for the railway at this time. 57xx Class 0-6-0PT 8737, one of the last batch with the earlier smaller-windowed cab, was shunting the goods yard at Tyseley on 29th August 1959. 863 of these pannier tanks were built, of which 16 have survived into preservation. 8737 had only arrived at Tyseley from Bristol St. Philip's Marsh in June 1959 and left for St. Blazey less than four months later.

A three-car Derby suburban DMU arriving at Tyseley on the Up Relief line with the 2.45pm Birmingham Moor Street-Stratford on Saturday 29th August 1959. This train will be taking the North Warwickshire line at the junction immediately beyond Tyseley station and stopped at all stations before reaching Stratford at 3.44pm. The North Warwickshire line, which is now marketed as the Shakespeare Line, had a narrow escape from closure in 1968 when notices for the replacement of the local trains on the line by a bus service were published, the long-distance services having been transferred in 1962 to the former Midland Railway route via the Lickey incline. Local residents had fought a battle against this since 1966 and after the final closure procedure was botched in April 1969 the line remained open following the granting of an injunction by the Court of Appeal in May 1969 on the day before the final trains were scheduled to run. Fifteen years elapsed before British Rail made an attempt to remove the injunction and close the section between Henley-in-Arden and Stratford, but this too was defeated by local opposition and today there is an hourly service each way throughout the day serving 16 intermediate stations between Birmingham and Stratford.

Collett Hall class 4-6-0 5909 *Newton Hall* with the 9.35am Saturdays Only Swansea High Street-Birmingham Snow Hill which will have come off the North Warwickshire line was passing Tyseley over an hour late on Saturday 29th August 1959. 5909 was a Llanelly-shedded engine, so local spotters would have been pleased to see it. Tyseley station has the familiar layout of two wide island platforms and the overbridge, on which the booking hall is situated, carries Wharfedale Road. In the background is an engineering department converted Toad brake van together with a motorised trolley and other engineers' paraphernalia.

Wolverhampton Stafford Road's King 4-6-0 6017 *King Edward IV* approaches Tyseley station on the Up main with the 11.45am Birkenhead Woodside-Paddington on Saturday 29th August 1959. This left Snow Hill at 3.0pm and was due to arrive at Paddington at 5.15pm, having called at Leamington Spa and Banbury. The leading coach is a GWR Collett 1930s third followed by a BR Mark 1 brake second and an LMS third. Behind 6017 is Tyseley's large goods warehouse where an unsuccessful attempt had been made to paint out the GWR signage and it was still possible to read the second line: EXPRESS GOODS SERVICES - ONE DAY TRANSITS.

During the summer holiday period, the North Warwickshire line via Stratford, Honeybourne and Cheltenham provided a useful alternative route to Devon and Cornwall as well as South Wales. Tyseley Modified Hall 6971 *Athelhampton Hall* was passing through Shirley station with the 3.45pm Birmingham Snow Hill-Swansea High Street on Saturday 29th August 1959. Most services from Snow Hill to Cardiff and Swansea via Stratford-upon-Avon had been operated by DMU sets since 1957 but steam-hauled trains continued on summer Saturdays when greater passenger numbers needed longer formations. The train is made up of a mixture of BR, LMS and GWR coaching stock in both 'blood and custard' and maroon liveries. In the 1950s, most suburban stations still had their own goods yard and shed. Goods facilities at Shirley ceased in May 1968 and the site is now occupied by a builders' merchant.

The overbridge at Shirley station afforded excellent views of Down trains as they approached. In this picture 4930 *Hagley Hall* heads the 10.12am return holiday train from Ilfracombe to Wolverhampton Low Level on Saturday 29th August 1959. 4930 was a Taunton engine from May 1958 until October 1959 when it moved to Cardiff Canton. After withdrawal in December 1963, it arrived at Woodham Bros. scrapyard at Barry in June 1964, leaving in 1973 when it was sold to the Severn Valley Railway where it was restored and returned to operation there in 1979. In the following years until 1986, 4930 also often worked on main line specials. It was then stored until 1999 before going on static display at McArthurGlen shopping centre in Swindon. On its return to the Severn Valley in 2007 it began an extensive overhaul and did not return to traffic until 2022. It is the oldest surviving Hall 4-6-0 and is regarded as the Severn Valley's 'flagship', especially since the actual Hagley Hall is only a few miles from the railway's terminus at Kidderminster.

A three-car Derby high-density suburban DMU working the 5.20pm Henley-in-Arden to Birmingham Snow Hill service approaches Shirley station on Saturday 29th August 1959, passing a new housing development which was conveniently close to the station. Henley-in-Arden was the most important intermediate station on the North Warwickshire line and some of the local services terminated and returned from there, as in this case. Note in the foreground the refuge siding which was used to accommodate the stock and engine of the short working Birmingham to Shirley trains whilst turning around.

A measure of the busy holiday traffic from the West Country to the Birmingham area was that at Stratford-on-Avon in the late afternoon between 3.40pm and 7.8pm there were eleven expresses to Birmingham: three trains from Penzance together with one starting at St. Austell, one from Newquay, one from Kingswear and two from Paignton, two from Ilfracombe and one from Weston-Super-Mare. However, the days of extensive holiday traffic by rail vanished quickly as motor car ownership grew during the early 1960s. 4991 *Cobham Hall* approaches the Haslucks Green Road bridge at Shirley with the 10.55am Ilfracombe-Wolverhampton on Saturday 29th August 1959. The northbound expresses passed Shirley at speed having disposed of their bankers at Earlswood Lakes five miles to the south. 4991, like 4930 on page 99, was a Taunton engine, and both Halls would have taken over there from 43xx Class 2-6-0s which had brought their trains via the now-closed GWR Barnstaple-Taunton line.

Looking resplendent repainted in lined green livery newly applied by Swindon Works earlier in the month, BR Standard Class 4 4-6-0 75025 was restarting the 5.45pm Birmingham Snow Hill-Worcester Shrub Hill from Shirley station on Saturday 29th August 1959. The train ran via Stratford and Honeybourne, where it gained the Oxford, Worcester and Wolverhampton line (the "Old Worse and Worse") to continue to Evesham and Worcester. It was a fast businessmen's commuter service which ran non-stop to Shirley, then called at selected stations to Stratford before continuing via Honeybourne to Evesham. Note the Hawksworth post-war design First at the front of the train. 75025 was built at Swindon in 1954 and was allocated to Worcester depot between November 1957 and January 1964 except for a few months at Machynlleth in late 1960.

A three-car Derby-built suburban DMU with the 6.10pm Birmingham Moor Street to Henley-in-Arden shortly after leaving Shirley station on Saturday 29th August 1959. When Snow Hill station was rebuilt in the early 1900s it was not economic to widen the two-track tunnel entering the station from the south in the way that its northern approaches were improved and so Moor Street station was built at the south end of the tunnel to reduce the traffic passing through and to handle local commuter traffic originating from Leamington and the North Warwickshire line. The first Moor Street terminus was opened in July 1909 although the station we know today was only brought in to use in January 1914 after the completion of extensive engineering works to increase the capacity of the approach lines and to construct the goods depot.

Ex-Midland Railway three-cylinder compound 4-4-0 1000 with a Stephenson Locomotive Society special to Doncaster and York was waiting at platform 7, Birmingham New Street, on Sunday 30th August 1959. This was the original Johnson compound of 1902, rebuilt in 1914 under R. M. Deeley with a superheated G9AS boiler. It was withdrawn in 1951 and languished in the paint shop at Crewe, before being restored to 1914 condition and working order at Derby in 1959. This was its first major outing and it subsequently worked enthusiasts' specials on the main line until 1962. After spending twelve years in Clapham Museum, 1000 was transferred to the National Railway Museum in 1975 where it was overhauled and ran on the main lines of British Rail until 1983 before being retired, again, in the NRM. These engines, as well as the similar ones built by the LMS, were certainly attractive, especially in the opulent crimson lake livery. Because the later LMS Compounds were widely distributed throughout the system, they came to be known by enthusiasts as "Crimson Ramblers".

Stanier Class 5 4-6-0 45013 arriving at platform 9, Birmingham New Street on Sunday 30th August 1959 with stock for the 9.35am excursion to Rhyl, a popular holiday destination for Birmingham people. It was passing New Street No.2 signal box which was built by the LNWR in 1885. With the expansion of the station, it was later extended and became responsible for movements at the Derby end of the station's Midland side. The old New Street was really two stations, the LNWR side (platforms 1-6) and the Midland side (platforms 7-11), separated by a road called Queens Drive. Normally, trains for north Wales departed from the LNWR side, but in this case, it may have been using the Midland side because there were no available platforms on the LNWR side. Alternatively, some excursion trains started at Kings Norton on the Midland line to the south-west, and since it is arriving at the east end of the station, it may have travelled from there via the Camp Hill line.

The 12.50pm Birmingham New Street-Coventry, composed of a two-car Gloucester Carriage & Wagon Co. set (later Class 100) and a two-car Metro-Cammell unit, was arriving at Stechford on Saturday 5th September 1959. The GC&W unit with Driving Motor Brake Second M50354 leading and Driving Trailer Composite M56109 trailing, was one of nine units transferred from Brunswick in Liverpool to Walsall Ryecroft depot in June 1958, as evidenced by the painted '3C' shed code on the cowling adjacent to the front buffer beam. It is in the original multiple unit livery of malachite green with cream lining, but without 'speed whiskers'. It would later receive the darker green like the Metro-Cammell unit it is attached to.

Castle Bromwich was on the north-eastern outskirts of Birmingham, and its station was on the former Midland Railway from Birmingham New Street to Derby. Here, ex-LMS Horwich Mogul 42759 was passing through with the 12.45pm Bristol Temple Meads-Sheffield Midland on Saturday 5th September 1959. 42759, built at Crewe Works in 1927, was allocated to Burton-on-Trent from January 1959, having been at Cricklewood for the previous decade. The use of one of these 2-6-0s, popularly known as 'Crabs', on such a long-distance passenger train was confined to summer Saturdays when they were often employed on holiday relief trains. Castle Bromwich had an attractive station building on the overbridge carrying the Chester Road, and in addition to local Birmingham to Derby and Nuneaton/Leicester trains it was used by the service to Walsall via Sutton Park. Its main claim to fame was as the station for visitors to the annual British Industries Fair which was a showcase for British manufacturing and was held at Castle Bromwich for two weeks every year from 1920 until 1959. The station closed in 1968 but there are plans to re-open it.

In the 1950s long-distance passenger traffic on the important North East–South West route through Birmingham was dominated by Stanier Jubilees and Class 5 4-6-0s. BR Standard Class 5 4-6-0 73028 with an Up express (on ex-Midland lines 'Up' means towards Derby), passes Jubilee 45690 *Leander* hauling the 12.52pm York-Bristol Temple Meads at Castle Bromwich station on Saturday 5th September 1959. 73028 was allocated to Bath Green Park between May 1958 and June 1960. *Leander* had been a Bristol Barrow Road engine since September 1947 and was a regular on this route. Happily, it is still with us, having been rescued from Woodham Bros. Barry Docks scrap yard in 1972 and is currently operational on the main line.

Castle Class 4-6-0 5089 *Westminster Abbey* heads the 3.20pm Wolverhampton Low Level-Paddington at Chapel Lane, Lapworth on Sunday 6th September 1959. This train ran via Oxford, reaching Paddington at 6.55pm. The first three coaches are BR Mark 1s, of which the third is a restaurant car, and the remainder except another Mark 1 are ex-GWR of varying types. 5089 was one of the new Castles built in 1937-40 which, for accountancy reasons, were officially classified as rebuilds of withdrawn Star Class 4-6-0s. Numbered 5083-92, they were named after abbeys, except for 5086 *Viscount Horne*. 5089 entered service in November 1939 replacing Star 4069 which had been withdrawn in October 1939. It was allocated to Wolverhampton Stafford Road from May 1958 until the shed closed in September 1963 and then went to the freight shed at Oxley, from where it was withdrawn in November 1964.

A three-car Derby suburban DMU was working the 4.30pm Leamington Spa-Wellington at Chapel Lane, Lapworth on Sunday 6th September 1959. The unit is in its original unlined green livery with 'speed whiskers' and has only one windscreen wiper (units were later fitted with an additional one on the 'secondman's' side). Lapworth originally opened as Kingswood but was renamed in May 1902 to avoid confusion (as if there would be any!) with a station of the same name in Surrey. The line from Birmingham to Lapworth was quadrupled in 1933 but has since reverted to double track.

Another three-car Derby suburban DMU with the 4.20pm Birmingham Moor Street-Leamington Spa at Chapel Lane, Lapworth on Sunday 6th September 1959. After Lapworth, it will call at Hatton and Warwick before reaching Leamington at 5.8pm.

A fine action shot of Hall 4-6-0 5912 *Queen's Hall* hauling the 4.10pm Paddington-Birkenhead Woodside near Rowington Junction, just south of Lapworth, on Sunday 6th September 1959. 5912, a Tyseley engine since June 1952, was unusual motive power for a direct Birkenhead service, the mixed traffic engine perhaps being employed because it was a Sunday. Rowington Junction was originally the junction of a branch line to Henley-in-Arden, opened in 1894, but soon usurped by the opening of the North Warwickshire Railway's station there in 1908. The junction layout changed over the years and the branch was later closed. At the time of the picture all that remained were two sidings used either to store surplus stock or crippled wagons, operated from a ground frame that had in October 1957 replaced the junction's signal box. The ground frame, junction and sidings were all taken out of service in 1968.

5025 *Chirk Castle* arriving at Lapworth station on Sunday 6th September 1959. The headlamp indicates a stopping passenger train and, indeed it was, the 4.5pm Wolverhampton-Oxford semi-fast which called at all stations to Leamington Spa except Widney Manor, rather a menial task for such an engine. After ten years at Bristol Bath Road, 5025 was transferred to Oxford in March 1958, so it was probably working home; it had been paired with a Hawksworth flat-sided tender since February 1959. Lapworth station, with its two wide platforms had island platform buildings and canopies of the same design as those at Solihull, Knowle & Dorridge, Acocks Green, Tyseley and Bordesley.

At Stechford station Stanier 8F 2-8-0 48501 was about to couple up to the wagons before setting off tender-first with a freight onto the Aston line, which diverged to the right, on Monday 7th September 1959. 48501 was allocated to Heaton Mersey shed at Stockport from June 1955 until withdrawn in July 1967, so it may have been heading back to the north west. Although an LMS design, this engine was built by the LNER at Darlington Works in June 1944 and was on loan to the LNER until October 1946.

Hawksworth Modified Hall 6971 *Athelhampton Hall* with an Up Class K freight at the Down end of Solihull station on Tuesday 8th September 1959. 6971 entered service in October 1947 and was allocated to Tyseley in August 1950, staying there until withdrawn in October 1964. It was originally paired with a Hawksworth straight-sided tender, but this had been replaced with a Collett tender.

WD Austerity 2-8-0 90403 heads an Up Class H freight from Woodcock Lane overbridge, near Acocks Green and South Yardley station, on Tuesday 8th September 1959.

Acocks Green, which was the first station on the Paddington line after the junction at Tyseley, is just visible in the distance.

These locomotives, intended for military use, in World War Two were designed for the Ministry of Supply by Robert Riddles and introduced in 1943. In 1948 British Railways purchased 733 of them together with a further 25 of the similar 2-10-0s.

90403, unusually working on the Up Main line, was allocated to the former Great Central shed at Woodford Halse from December 1954 and was probably working home via Banbury.

One of the ubiquitous three-car Derby suburban DMUs with the 1.20pm Birmingham Moor Street-Leamington had just left Acocks Green and South Yardley on the Up Relief line on Tuesday 8th September 1959.

Branching off on the extreme left of the picture is the beginning of the Down goods loop. This route was used by many freight trains, including slow-moving iron ore trains, and they were frequently held in this loop while waiting to negotiate the junction at Tyseley.

King Class 4-6-0 6024 *King Edward I* with the 2.35pm Birkenhead Woodside-Paddington at Hillfield Road bridge near Widney Manor on Tuesday 8th September 1959. It had been fitted with a double chimney during a Heavy General overhaul completed in March 1957. 6024 was one of the two Kings preserved after spending more than a decade at Barry Docks scrapyard and was restored at Quainton Road by the '6024 Preservation Society'. It returned to the main line in 1990 and made history by working into Cornwall in May 1998 with the "The Par King Pioneer" special. 6024 was sold in 2011 to the Royal Scot Locomotive and General Trust, chaired by investor and steam enthusiast Jeremy Hosking, and since then has been under overhaul to main line condition by the '6024 Preservation Society' who remain responsible for its care.

British Railways Standard 9F 2-10-0 92152 was heading a northbound Class D part-fitted freight at the underbridge near Widney Manor station on Tuesday 8th September 1959. This was probably an inter-regional working, its most likely destination being Washwood Heath Sidings in Birmingham, which it would reach via Bordesley Junction. 92152 is in filthy external condition, with a considerable build-up of lime scale on the boiler. It was built at Crewe in October 1957, allocated to Saltley depot and was withdrawn in November 1967 after only ten years in service.

Two three-car Derby suburban DMUs work the 6.48pm Lapworth Spa-Wellington near Widney Manor on Tuesday 8th September 1959. Not all local trains on this route started or terminated at Leamington and some, like this one, originated at Lapworth. Today the most common terminating station is Dorridge (formerly Knowle & Dorridge), from which trains now run via Birmingham Snow Hill to Kidderminster or Worcester. As with the earlier picture of this service on page 86, the destination board shows Birmingham Snow Hill.

The 5.00pm Leamington Spa-Birmingham Moor Street in the form of a three-car Derby suburban DMU was arriving at Acocks Green on the Down Main on Wednesday 9th September 1959. When this section of the line was quadrupled in 1906-07, the station was completely rebuilt, with wide island platforms and standard GWR buildings. The footbridge gave access to the surrounding suburban roads and was used mainly by season ticket holders. If one needed to buy a ticket, it was necessary to use the ticket office at the main entrance on Sherbourne Road. The tall poplar trees, which were a feature of the photographs taken from the Woodcock Lane overbridge, can be seen in the distance.

Hockley, the first station out of Birmingham Snow Hill heading towards Wolverhampton and reached after passing through Hockley tunnel, was unusual in having no platform on the Down Main line. Old Oak Common's 6010 *King Charles I* was passing on Thursday 10th September 1959 with the 2.35pm Birkenhead Woodside-Paddington which the King would have taken over at Wolverhampton. The destination board on the leading coach reads 'Paddington-Birmingham-Shrewsbury'; it should have been reversed! Alongside Hockley station there was a large goods station; the 25 ton gantry crane of the Up side goods yard (or 'Round' Yard) is visible behind the train.

At the Western Region's Wolverhampton Low Level station on Saturday 12th September 1959, King 4-6-0 6009 *King Charles II* backs on to the 11.45am Birkenhead Woodside-Paddington. The Birkenhead trains were hauled by a smaller 4-6-0, usually a Hall, County, or Castle between Chester and Wolverhampton, and they were usually worked by a tank engine between Birkenhead and Chester. 6009 was only ever allocated to Old Oak Common, from new in March 1928 until withdrawal in September 1962.

Hampton-in-Arden lies to the south-east of Birmingham on the New Street-Coventry line. Jubilee 4-6-0 45567 *South Australia* was passing through the station (which is the other side of Bridge No.346, hidden by the train) with the 1.28pm Wolverhampton High Level-Euston on Sunday 13th September 1959. 45567 was allocated to Edge Hill shed, Liverpool, so perhaps it was being borrowed by Bushbury shed, which usually worked these trains. In the foreground is the Down goods loop, which ended with a head-shunt just before the bridge, which allowed passenger trains to overtake slow-moving freights. The 13th should have been the last day of express services between Euston, New Street and Wolverhampton High Level with these trains withdrawn to permit electrification work on the route. But a widespread strike in the printing industry meant new timetables could not be produced and the change was deferred until 2nd November. From that date additional trains were provided by the Western Region between Paddington, Snow Hill and Wolverhampton Low Level.

On Sundays, the London and Birmingham line between Rugby and Stechford was frequently used as a diversionary route when there was engineering work on the Trent Valley line through Nuneaton, Tamworth and Lichfield, especially during the electrification of the West Coast Main Line when it would often be completely closed. At Stechford diverted trains would take the line to Aston, where they would join the Grand Junction route towards Stafford. Royal Scot 4-6-0 46162 *Queen's Westminster Rifleman* was approaching Bridge 346 and Hampton-in-Arden station with a northbound diverted train on Sunday 13th September 1959. 46162 from Camden shed was one of the 1930 Derby-built batch of Royal Scots. It was rebuilt with a 2A boiler in 1948 and in the same year participated in the Locomotive Interchange Trials where it produced extremely positive results when competing against the Pacific classes from other Regions tested against it in the Express Passenger category. The freight, in the Down goods loop hauled by an 8F 2-8-0 with a Fowler 3,500 gallon tender, was possibly a permanent way train.

The 2.35pm Birmingham New Street-Coventry departing from Hampton-in-Arden on Sunday 13th September 1959 was formed of a two-car Park Royal unit (Class 103 under TOPS) ahead of a two-car Metro-Cammell unit. The Park Royal unit was in original, light green, livery with no 'speed whiskers'. The leading vehicle is Driving Trailer Composite M56153 and the rear vehicle of the unit is Driving Motor Brake Second M50398. The unit had entered service in February 1958, allocated to Llandudno Junction and was transferred to Walsall Ryecroft the following May as part of the 'Birmingham Part 2' dieselisation scheme, replacing steam on local services in the area. The original Hampton-in-Arden station had been slightly closer to Birmingham, but the LNWR built a new station on the present site in 1884.

Berkswell was the next station on the New Street-Euston line after Hampton-in-Arden. Camden's Jubilee 4-6-0 45624 *St. Helena* with the 4.10pm Birmingham New Street-Euston, was passing through and over its level crossing on Sunday 13th September 1959. The train was slowing for the junction signal which controlled access to the short cut-off which joined the Coventry to Leamington line at Kenilworth Junction. This closed in 1965, so that trains for Leamington now have to go via Coventry. Nearer the camera, the track diverging to the right led to the small goods yard. When the goods yard closed one siding was retained and used for many years as an 'overnight' stabling siding for the Royal Train when members of the Royal Family were visiting the West Midlands.

Two single unit diesel cars, W55004 and W55005, were waiting with the 4.00pm to Birmingham Snow Hill at Dudley on Saturday 26th September 1959. After withdrawal in 1992, W55005 was preserved and is currently based on the Battlefield Line in Leicestershire. Before the introduction of the 'Bubble Cars' the Dudley-Snow Hill service, known as "The Dudley Dodger", was usually worked by ex-GWR streamlined diesel railcars, which had themselves replaced steam auto-trains powered by 0-4-2Ts. Dudley, a joint station with separate platforms for the LNWR/LMS and GWR trains, was closed in 1964 and became a Freightliner terminal (itself closed in 1989) and is now the site of the Very Light Rail National Innovation Centre which was opened in September 2022.

A three-car Swindon-built Cross-Country DMU passes Priestfield on Saturday 26th September 1959 with the 4.3pm Birmingham Snow Hill-Wolverhampton Low Level, probably a filling-in turn since it was allocated to Cardiff Canton at this date. It then ran to Cosford, an unusual terminating point, before return to Wolverhampton Low Level at 5.16pm. The tracks in the foreground joining the main line were those of the former Oxford Worcester and Wolverhampton Railway route south to Stourbridge Junction via Dudley which lost its services in July 1962. Services between Wolverhampton Low Level and Birmingham Snow Hill ceased on 6th March 1972, but the West Midlands Metro between Birmingham and Wolverhampton returned a rail presence to Priestfield in 1999; the tram stop here is the last before the street running section into Wolverhampton.

Stanier Class 8F 2-8-0 48415 passes through Priestfield station with a Down Class F unfitted freight on Saturday 26th September 1959. It was one of the class built by the GWR at Swindon Works during the war and was on loan to the GWR at Croes Newydd until May 1947 when it went to the LMS at Cricklewood. It would return to the Western in July 1956 at Pontypool Road when the region needed more 2-8-0s and British Railways sensibly turned down a request to build more of the GWR Collett 38xx 2-8-0s, transferring a number of the LMS design instead. The vacuum ejectors had to be repositioned from the normal position in front of the cab when they were fitted with GWR ATC equipment to avoid a problem which occurred if the driver did not cancel a warning when passing a distant signal at caution whereby a control valve on the ejector shut off steam to the ejector. 48415 was transferred to Tyseley in April 1959, moved to Saltley in February 1961, then Stourbridge Junction and back to Tyseley before finally withdrawal from Oxley shed in August 1966. Oxley was a satellite of nearby Stafford Road and housed mainly freight engines, the passenger locomotives being dealt with at Stafford Road, and was one of the last strongholds of Western Region steam.

Another view of Stafford Road's Castle 4-6-0 5089 *Westminster Abbey* (see page 109), this time with the 11.45am Birkenhead Woodside-Paddington at Wadleys Road, Solihull on Sunday 27th September 1959.

Michael was positioned on a small overbridge on the Birmingham side of Solihull, in an area worryingly known as Worlds End.

In 1842 the Birmingham & Derby Junction Railway opened a line from Birmingham to meet its existing line from Hampton-in-Arden to Derby at Whitacre. The latter lost its strategic importance with the opening of the Midland Counties route from Rugby to Leicester and Derby and was finally closed in 1930. In 1909 the Midland Railway had opened a cut-off from Water Orton rejoining the original line just south of Kingsbury, by-passing Whitacre and its awkward 'dogleg' completely. Standing near a footbridge over the new line just to the east of the junction at Water Orton, Michael photographed Horwich-built 8F 2-8-0 48381 from Wellingborough shed hauling a Toton to Washwood Heath Class H freight on Friday 2nd October 1959. In the background is Hams Hall power station, developed by the City of Birmingham Electricity Supply Department in 1929 and taken over by the state in 1948. The three coal-fired power stations there are long closed and today it is the site of Hams Hall Distribution Park, a large logistics centre that has a rail connection from the Whitacre line.

On the same footpath as the previous photograph, but a few yards to the south, another footbridge crosses the original Whitacre line. Midland Railway-built Fowler 4F 0-6-0 43863 was approaching the junction with the direct line from Derby and Tamworth at Water Orton with a Class J freight conveying more coal for Birmingham on Friday 2nd October 1959. 43863 was for many years allocated to Staveley (Barrow Hill) and was withdrawn from there in September 1961.

Hawksworth Modified Hall 4-6-0 7903 *Foremarke Hall* from Old Oak Common shed accelerates away from the junction at Tyseley on Sunday 18th October 1959 with the 8.10am Shrewsbury-Paddington and, with a leisurely Sunday schedule, was not due at Paddington until 12.40pm. The photograph was taken from the bridge carrying Stockfield Road over the Paddington line. In the distance is an 0-6-0PT on a short Class J freight and beyond it the North Warwickshire line diverges to the left with Tyseley South signal box controlling the junction. On the skyline, above the rear of the train, is the imposing Tyseley station entrance building situated on the Wharfdale Road overbridge. Beyond that, but not visible in this photograph, were the carriage sidings and Tyseley engine shed, now the Birmingham Railway Museum. 7903, which had retained its original straight-sided tender, was built in April 1949 and spent most of its career allocated to Old Oak Common shed. After withdrawal in June 1964, it went to Woodham Bros. scrapyard at Barry Docks and was rescued from there in 1981. Restoration to working order took until 2003 and today 7903 works on the Gloucestershire Warwickshire Steam Railway.

Photographed from the Streetsbrook Road overbridge just to the north of Solihull, Old Oak Common King 6022 *King Edward III* was heading the 8.5am Birkenhead Woodside-Paddington on Sunday 18th October 1959. The large numerals in the frame attached to the smokebox door indicated the identity of the train to signalmen. 6022 had been an Old Oak Common engine since 1955 but was transferred to Stafford Road in July 1959 and was withdrawn from there in September 1962.

Sunday is traditionally the day for maintenance work on the railway. On Sunday 18th October 1959, Hawksworth Class 94xx 0-6-0PT 9474 was heading a permanent way train on the Up Relief line at Streetsbrook Road, approaching Solihull. The headshunt from Solihull goods depot is the furthest line on the right. 9474, which was one of a batch of the Hawksworth pannier tanks built in Newcastle by Robert Stephenson & Hawthorn between 1950 and 1953, was officially listed as allocated to Exeter shed at the date of this photograph, and was transferred to Wolverhampton Oxley in July 1960; it was withdrawn in November 1961 after less than ten years in service.

In another photograph taken from the Woodcock Lane overbridge near Acocks Green and South Yardley station, which is just visible in the distance, Hall class 4-6-0 4951 *Pendeford Hall* was on the Up Main with a Class D fitted freight on Monday 19th October 1959. 4951 was allocated to Oxley shed between February 1957 and October 1962. The train has a wonderful mix of vehicle types with a variety of four-wheel vans interspersed with bogie GUVs. To the left of the picture is the Down goods loop and its associated head-shunt.

A week after the picture of it on page 135, 6022 *King Edward III* at the Streetsbrook Road bridge at Solihull, was re-starting from a signal check and was working the same train, the 8.5am Birkenhead Woodside-Paddington, on Sunday 25th October 1959. The cylinder drain cocks are open and there is a whisp of steam above the whistle.

The RCTS Photograph Collection

The Society owns the rights to various collections of original slides, negatives and prints which have been donated or bequeathed to the Society. Many, but by no means all, have been digitised and captioned and are available to view and purchase.

Approximately 57,000 images are available via *Search and Buy*. The spreadsheet-like tool enables you to find specific imagery or simply browse. A random selection of images will be selected each time you open the screen. The full-resolution images are available to view with watermarks (an RCTS logo and a grid overlay) and can be zoomed and panned.

All of the images in this book have been taken from this archive. Please visit our website rcts.org.uk to view the collection. It is found under the sub-heading *The RCTS Digital Archive*.

SEARCH and BUY

10% off when spending £30.00 or more on photographs (not other items) with coupon code S6PKCPVU.

All images are available as JPG downloads (£2.00 each) or as standard 6x4 gloss prints (£2.50 each). They are supplied with a caption strip at the bottom containing the collection name, a reference code and the caption. A small RCTS logo is on the bottom right.

There is a minimum shipping order of £5.00 (excluding shipping for prints) — that is, three three digital downloads or two prints. Prints can be shipped to UK addresses for which there is a standard charge of £3.00 irrespective of quantity. Other items from the Digital Archive can be added to your basket to make up the £5.00. Coupons offering discounts may be available at various times.

Other print options (including non-UK shipping) are available from our print supplier *One Vision Imaging Ltd.* of Coventry. Purchase digital downloads from the RCTS, then upload them to One Vision's portal. Other print options include larger sizes up to 45x30, alternate finishes (including fine art), framing, photo books etc.

Locomotives of the Great Western Railway

The Books

A definite locomotive history, such as the 14-part *Locomotives of the Great Western Railway* deserves to be readily accessible. It took 42 years (1951-93) to complete the series with several parts reprinted but, there was never a time when all 14 parts were in print together. it is now possible to use digital print-to-order and online services to overcame the (mostly economic) limitations of litho print technology to make the full series available at the same time.

The could originally be collected as a part-work, if you were patient. We have chosen to group the c.1,950 pages of text and photographs into three larger volumes of 500 to 740 pages in length. The grouping is logical rather than chronological.

Numerous updates and corrections were published in Parts 12, 13 and 14. These have been redistributed to be co-located with the original part. A facsimile is not able to match the production standards of a modern original but, we have done our best. The text has been whitened, blemishes removed and half-tone images processed into pixels.

The Society President, Rev, Canon Brian Arman, has written a forword which appears in every volume or file.

Again, please visit our website rcts.org.uk to view this series of books. It is also found under the sub-heading *The RCTS Digital Archive.*

Digital Downloads

Searchable PDF files are available to download at £12.00 each for the following years:

- Volume 1 incorporating Parts 1, 12, 13 and 14
- Volume 2 incorporating Parts 2, 3 and 10
- Volume 3 incorporating Parts 4 to 9 and 11.

Important: For contents, please read the product descriptions carefully as some sections in the originals have been moved.

For £30.00, a bundle of all 14 parts (as seperate files) is available, a saving of £6.00.

Printed Books

The following books are available to purchase from Amazon in all the countries they serve. Prices are £25.00-£30.00 each from Amazon UK or the equivalent in local currency elsewhere plus VAT where applicable.

All volumes are available to order. Please check on Amazon UK for further details.

- Volume 1 (£25)
- Volume 2 (£30)
- Volume 3 (£30)

CURRENT TITLES IN OUR CATALOGUE AS AT APRIL 2024

BR Standard Steam Locomotives	ISBN	Retail (£)
Vol. 1 The Pacific Classes and Introduction (reprint)	978-0-9934908-6-6	19.00
Vol. 2 The 4-6-0 and 2-6-0 Classes	978-0-901115-93-5	19.00
Vol. 3 The Tank Engine Classes (reprint)	978-0-9934908-5-9	19.00
Vol. 4 The 9F 2-10-0 Class (reprint)	978-0-901115-95-9	27.50
Vol. 5 The End of an Era	978-0-901115-97-3	19.00

Locomotives of the LMS

The Hughes and Stanier 2-6-0s	978-0-901115-96-6	16.00
The Jubilee 4-6-0s (updated)	978-0-901115-94-2	20.00
Raising Steam on the LMS	978-0-901115-85-0	6.50
L&NWR Locomotive Names	978-0-901115-90-4	8.00
The Stanier Class Five 4-6-0s Volume 1	978-0-901115-98-0	20.00
The Stanier Class Five 4-6-0s Volume 2	978-0-901115-99-7	20.00
The Stanier Pacifics	978-0-9934908-0-4	22.50
The Patriot 4-6-0s	978-0-9934908-1-1	20.00
The Royal Scot 4-6-0s	978-0-9934908-7-3	29.50

Locomotives of the LNER

We have scanned all 19 books in this series as the original copies were all out-of-print. They are now available in several formats. There is free online browsing and PDF downloads to purchase at *https://archive.rcts.org.uk/*. Amazon offers facsimile books, consolidated into 8 parts.

Non Series Books

THE JOURNEY	978-0-9934908-2-8	10.00
Brush Diesel & Electric Locomotives 1980-2020	978-0-9934908-3-5	20.00
Michael Mensing – Railway Photographer	978-0-9934908-4-2	17.50
A Photographic Journey 1980-2020 – John Cowlishaw	978-0-9934908-8-0	19.95
Observing the Railway in 2022	978-0-9934908-9-7	25.00
An illustrated History of First Generations DMUs	978-1-7391324-0-8	25.00

Purchase via our website rcts.org.uk or alternatively by post from
RCTS Sales, 16 Welby Close, Maidenhead SL6 3PY
Cheques payable to RAILWAY CORRESPONDENCE & TRAVEL SOCIETY
For all orders please add £4.00 P/P.